Sophie Bryant

The Teaching of Morality in the Family and the School

Sophie Bryant

The Teaching of Morality in the Family and the School

ISBN/EAN: 9783337000127

Printed in Europe, USA, Canada, Australia, Japan

Cover: Foto ©Suzi / pixelio.de

More available books at **www.hansebooks.com**

THE TEACHING OF MORALITY.

The volumes of the series already published are :—

CIVILIZATION OF CHRISTENDOM, and other Studies. By BERNARD BOSANQUET, M.A. (Oxon.), LL.D. (Glasgow). 4s. 6d.

SHORT STUDIES IN CHARACTER. By SOPHIE BRYANT, D.Sc. (Lond.). 4s. 6d.

SOCIAL RIGHTS AND DUTIES. By LESLIE STEPHEN. 2 vols. 9s.

THE TEACHING OF MORALITY IN THE FAMILY AND THE SCHOOL. By SOPHIE BRYANT, D.Sc. (Lond.). 3s.

Other volumes to follow by

Professor A. SIDGWICK, Professor D. G. RITCHIE, and J. H. MUIRHEAD (The Editor).

The Ethical Library

THE TEACHING OF MORALITY

IN

THE FAMILY AND THE SCHOOL

BY

SOPHIE BRYANT, D.Sc.

HEAD MISTRESS OF THE NORTH LONDON COLLEGIATE SCHOOL FOR GIRLS, AUTHOR OF
"EDUCATIONAL ENDS" AND "STUDIES IN CHARACTER," ETC.

London
SWAN SONNENSCHEIN & CO., Limited
NEW YORK: THE MACMILLAN CO.
1897

To
F. M. B.

PREFACE.

In the following pages I have attempted rather to suggest than to describe the procedure appropriate to instruction in morality. The part played by such instruction in the whole system of moral education is first considered, and the application of the general principles of good teaching to this particular kind of teaching is later discussed. In the first and second chapters there will be found some analysis of the intellectual and instinctive processes involved in the successful pursuit of moral wisdom. Finally, the subject matter of lessons in morality is treated under the two supplementary heads of Virtuous Character and Social Membership.

I know that even now there are those who have doubts as to the efficiency of any definite instruction in the principles of the good life simply as such. Some hold that the good life can only be taught by living it, and that systematic reflection on the ideals implied in it are, in youth, more likely to be a hindrance than a help. Others believe that morality cannot be taught except as a sequel to religion, thus missing, as it seems to me, the full significance of the mutual relationship which both derive from the human need to see life whole and its meaning real. But, without entering into argument with doubters of either kind at this point, I would suggest to the reader the test of plain experience. My experience—based on some teaching to school girls between the ages of about twelve and eighteen—is (1) that young people are much interested in the ideas of right and wrong, (2) that they are apt to be impressed and effectively moved by that strain of moral reflection which shows the unity of virtue in all the variety of the virtues, and (3) that they acquire this kind of knowledge as naturally as any other, while they are apt to apply it with more interest and skill. With greater certainty, however, I can speak of the practical results of such teaching as given in the North London Collegiate School by my valued friend and leader, the late Miss Frances Mary Buss. As regards its permanency of effect and variety of application in later as well as in earlier life, the direct personal testimony of the learners is singularly abundant and convincing. Thus experience verifies that faith in the value of instruction in morality, which is founded on an estimate of the forces that regulate human character and life.

SOPHIE BRYANT.

HAMPSTEAD, *May*, 1897.

CONTENTS.

INTRODUCTION.
PAGE
MORAL EDUCATION IN GENERAL, - - - - - 1

CHAPTER I.
INTELLECTUAL PROCESSES INVOLVED IN THE STUDY OF MORALITY, - - - - - - - - 33

CHAPTER II.
MORALIZING INSTINCTS DEVELOPED BY THE STUDY OF MORALITY, - - - - - - - - 63

CHAPTER III.
PRINCIPLES OF TEACHING, - - - - - - 83

CHAPTER IV.
THE SUBJECT MATTER—VIRTUOUS CHARACTER, - - 108

CHAPTER V.
THE SUBJECT MATTER—SOCIAL MEMBERSHIP, - - 132

INTRODUCTION.

MORAL EDUCATION IN GENERAL.

It is a doubtful wisdom that begins a treatise with a definition, but we cannot well dispense with some preliminary statement of the end proposed in Moral Education. Otherwise there is danger that we may aim too low, or swerve sideways so as to miss the mark. We want more than the production of nicely behaved children, and we aim at the development of something not quite the same as orderly citizens, respectable men, or even useful members of society.

In what, then, does morality essentially consist? Morality, in the first place, is the steady recognition by a man of himself as an individual who ought to live according to some system of conduct which binds him equally with all his fellows. This steady recognition of the moral law, or duty, as binding, passes over into that constantly repeated preference for dutiful courses which is the good, or well and firmly directed, will. Thus the authoritative idea of duty determines that a limit shall be set to all impulses and desires, so that none shall be practically operative if inconsistent with it.

Character, being thus co-ordinated by the consciousness of this law of life, freely shapes itself according to the man's idea of duty. All those elements of his nature which are auxiliary to it—sympathy, faithfulness, truth, and the like—are pressed into service and wax strong; while the whole unsocial brood of malice, falsehood, and rampant selfishness suffer the consequences of continual trampling under foot. Thus dutifulness makes for the growth of a character in which duty is the natural unconstrained expression of personal disposition. And, on the other hand, the nurture by any means of such a personal disposition—self-respecting, sympathetic, reasonable—as is conformable to duty, tends to establish the consciousness of duty on a safer throne.

So far we have found in morality the familiar ideas of *conscience* and *virtuous disposition*, both finding expression in a system of life to be lived. Knowledge of this system, and judgment in applying it—these make *moral wisdom*, the third element in morality. It is necessary to understand the content of conscience, both in general precept and in particular application. This is a long work of experience, reflection, and practical judgment. Wisdom comes with the lapse of years, but only to those who set their heart on it early and search for it with care. The little child is often peculiarly clear in the sense of his need for more knowledge of good.

Thus is morality compounded; and yet it is not in truth compounded, but is simply the whole outcome of a will set upon good, from which emerges presently the completely formed character and rightly judging reason, expressing themselves in life as a free and finely fashioned will. But for our purpose it will prove useful to note the complexity of its development, since a great part of the educator's work consists in removing obstacles to that development. Thus we labour to "train character" in the sense of cultivating virtuous predispositions—amiable habits of mind. And likewise we engage in moral instruction, so filling the intellect with ideas of the good life as continually to urge the consciousness of duty to a more perfect activity.

The educator labours to assist in bringing about the full fruition of morality in the child. It is not enough that he should understand morality. He must understand how morality gets itself accomplished without his interference, and he must with much searchings of heart consider how his interference can be of use. His first step, therefore, will be to inquire how, and under what conditions, the good man most easily and certainly becomes himself, and likewise under what conditions he is likely to fail. It will then remain for him to see what part he can take in securing the presence of those conditions that make for success and the absence of all that tend to cause failure. Stimulus, sympathy, and example he will add as of course.

The child emerges in his world as a being disposed to activity *initiated* by himself, but disposed also to act from moment to moment on the ideas suggested by others. To realize this clearly, let us put before ourselves broadly the main fact that acts issue from the idea of the act, that, as a first approximation to the truth, it may be said that if the idea of an act for any reason arises vividly in the mind it tends to translate itself naturally into act. This being so, we must next ask whence and why the ideas of action come; and we are at once at the source of some of the most important varieties of individuality. There is suggestion simple from without, conveyed by words, by example, by gesture; and there is auto-suggestion from within. The impressionable child takes up at once the idea expressed by another in words—his imagination bodies it forth without resistance freely—he does what he is told without any particular sense of obedience in doing it. The imitative child is more specially susceptible to the idea suggested by an act of example: he is more instinctively dramatic perhaps than the other, that is, he combines with his imagination a larger share of undirected activity, and this fund of activity is immediately stirred by sympathy with the *expression* of another. Imitativeness and impressionability run into each other, though two central types may be distinguished. The one is moved by an idea as such, impressed in its wholeness and speciality on the imagination, while the other is affected more broadly by an impulse of vague sympathy towards identification with acts of a particular sort. Sometimes, as is well known, a child who resists impressions yields to the imitative impulse in a way that surprises those who have been impressed by his indocility. The explanation, however, is not far to seek. A child of this sort is one of the natural rebels, who receive instructions to act with a distinct counterflow of hostile ideas of their own, and who therefore do not act on these instructions without consciousness of obedience to some *superior* will. This consciousness they resent; but if the same instruction is presented, not as instruction but by example, the instinct of rebellion is not aroused and the act follows. The rebellious instinct may co-exist with much impressionability and much imitativeness; a positive resentment to any attempt to control the will is its root. A child of this type will do anything so long as he is not driven, but will not act without the subtle consciousness of his own initiative behind the act.

Distinguished from these is the child impervious to suggestion, who grows probably into the man inaccessible to ideas, doomed to an early descent into old fogeydom. This child seems to be most perversely disobedient when he is only impervious to the instructions given. It is not simply that his mind is set on suggestions proceeding from himself. His characteristic is that he is, for the greater part, accessible to such suggestions only, —that the suggestions of others produce the minimum of influence upon him. The normal mind accepts suggestions and works them up with its own previous ideas to regulate act. It is at once auto- and extra-suggestible. Streams from two sources flow together, the main stream of auto-suggestion determining action as it occurs, but being modified by the tributary stream of ideas suggested from without. The mind abnormally open to influence is so because of the poverty of its main stream: the tributary in that case becomes the river, and the course of the river is determined by the influx of tributaries. And on the other hand, the merely auto-suggestible, or inaccessible, mind is like a river flowing steadily along between high banks which permit no access of new streams into it.

It is not easy to over-estimate the importance to the morality of each individual of being in the normal mean thus defined, so far as the practical ideas which govern life are concerned. The three types are familiar in our experience of men : the man of steadfast character and reasonable mind, his ideas of right steady and clear, but capable of infinitely variable adaptation according to the physical and social requirements of the case. On either side of him stand the two faulty extremes—extreme because deficient, each in one or other of those two elements which make up the harmony and balance in him— on the one hand, the narrow man who can only see the path on which his own feeble lantern of original wisdom shines, on the other, the man too easily influenced, who is swayed hither and thither by every wind of feeling and opinion, having no solid root of preference or conviction in himself.

As in medicine so in education, the scientific art has two aims in view :—first, the preservation of such healthy conditions of life as shall make the production of the normal type probable; and secondly, the detection and proper diagnosis of unfavourable symptoms, with the adoption of remedial treatment corresponding. In good education every means is taken to develop, on the one hand, the child's natural dependence and insistence on his own initiative in action—his *moral originality*, as it might be called—, and to train him, on the other hand, to a high degree of susceptibility to the thoughts and feelings surrounding him—to *moral docility*, as this might be called. As in the intellectual, so in the moral life, originality and docility are alike indispensable. It is for education to establish conditions favourable to the development of both, and equally favourable as a rule. The educator, however, must do more than this for the exceptional cases of those who lean to one or other of the two extremes. First, he has to discover them; then to understand exactly what is the nature of their complaint; and lastly, he has to adjust his general treatment to them. Complex cases will occur, severely taxing his skill; but only general considerations can be touched on here. The morally indocile has to be trained to increase his docility, and this will be best done by attacking the fault in the intellectual quite as much as in the moral domain. The fault is difficult of treatment in the moral life, for the wheat may be pulled up with the tares. This will happen if we rely altogether on checking the child's active expression of his own ideas, in order to remind him that there are other interests to consider. This is the most obvious method of treatment, but a little reflection, as well as observation, shows that it is the worst—the worst, that is, of fairly reasonable methods. It is bad, because each time it is applied there is a check on the child's initiative to express himself in act. Action has already begun and is pulled up short. This must happen sometimes, and should, but a regular treatment of it is very enfeebling, and destroys the ability to act promptly and decidedly. A vigorous child resents such treatment, " will fight," and, I venture to say, " will be right." It is, above all things, essential to respect the child's initiative in action—his self-will, as parents and teachers call it. *The necessary modification of initiative should occur before it has reached the stage of pouring itself forth in action.*

I advise then that, in the treatment of the morally indocile or inaccessible, reliance be placed chiefly on the cultivation of docility in general intellectual work and in *theoretic* moral instruction. At the same time, let obedience not be despised. It is often an unattractive but always a necessary virtue. Its reasonableness is based on the actual necessary subordination of the individual to law and to his conditions, a hard fact which must be learned early; and the sooner it is accepted as the ground of a great moral virtue, and the occasion for the development of more virtue, the better for the child.[1] This hard fact of subordination is

---

[1] Be it remembered, too, that obedience to love is not pure obedience, and is therefore not enough.

learned through experience of checks to self-will, and therefore some checks are necessary to the learning of obedience. But my point is, that if we add to these a further series of checks aimed at indocility, (which differs from disobedience though allied to it,) we may seriously endanger vigour of will, which is the mainspring of character. Indocility and vigorous originality of will coincide perhaps more often than not, in which case much checking does no harm, but the wise parent can detect the signs of too little and too much. *There is too much when initiative droops and flags.*

Indocility is like a fever that makes itself seen, and obviously demands treatment. Defective initiative is much more likely to be neglected. To the average parent and the average teacher the easily influenced child is delightful so long as under good influences. Few delight in the merely receptive as friends: there is more companionship in a person who meets one's ideas with other ideas and stands up to his view of the case, though with courtesy and sympathy when opposite developments arise. But we have hardly learned to expect such companionability, even in its rudiments, from children. We are the losers thereby, because the very crudity and freshness of a child's original ideas make them very delightful; and the child is the loser, because we are apt to give him little encouragement. Most children, indeed, get into the way of keeping their ideas to themselves; or, at most, they communicate them only to one another. A worse result is that we actually tend to prefer the children who mostly reflect our ideas after their manner, and are easily led *by us*. The danger is obvious. The easily led child is the victim of influences: he grows into the easily led man, and the chances are great that he may fall under evil influences at some critical moment. And so it is that the naughty children, whose indocility and rebellion scandalize their respectable parents, often turn into better men than do the "dear little angels" who never opposed us in their lives. Children, indeed, considering the distance there is between our ideas and theirs, have no business to be so "good," unless all the people around them are very nearly perfect.

But even when the danger of the easily influenced child is recognized, his case is by no means easy to undertake. Everything must be done to encourage initiative, occasions invented on which the child is to choose what shall be done, and determine how to do it. In this case, the remedies are best applied in the practical field itself; the growth of original practical ideas even of the simplest sort, and their expression in act, has to be helped. Get such a child to lead a game, to plan an excursion, to choose his own books, to be secretary to a children's society, and you give him most genuine moral education. But at the same time, means to the same end may be taken in all the intellectual work, in all social converse, and in theoretic moral instruction most of all. On all sides encourage the formation of the child's ideas by the child: train him to *think* for himself, to entertain other people's thoughts—nay, to ponder them reverently—but in the long run to have all his knowledge and all his opinions in his mind as the product of his own thinking, the work of his own reason. This is moral training, and of the best kind. Place it in the background of the same kind of training in practical life—the training to *act in the long run out of one's own head*—and initiative must inevitably be strengthened through and through.

This acting out of one's own head in the idealist's sense must, of course, be clearly distinguished from the having one's own way of the unregenerate sensationalist, whose actions serve his natural personal desires and impulses only. Morality assumes these natural desires, and takes its start in the regulation and limitation of them by reference to an *idea* of order and suitability by which their proper exercise is defined. This is the Moral Idea, however crude and harsh may be its first outlines. It regulates, and, by regulating, sanctifies and refines the natural desires, and reduces their chaos to a cosmos over which it rules. *The first step in morality has not been taken till the idea of some moral order has asserted her rule over all active impulses.* If she does not, life remains at the level of the brute. Education must see to it above all else that this does not happen. The means consist in the quickening of reflection on conduct and its significance, in surrounding the child with an attractive idealizing atmosphere, in the constant presentation of the common relationships of life in a refined and sacred light, in the obvious existence of a social order within which he lives, and in the tacit assumption that this order must be maintained without exception.

Here, then, are three rules of expectation, for the fulfilment of which the born educator works:

(1) Expect the child to idealize conduct, that is, to bring all active impulses

under the control of ideas—to think about conduct.

(2) Expect the child to have his own ideas of conduct, and in the long run to act from them.

(3) Expect the child to treat all other people's ideas with respect, and some with reverence, and to be ready to try his own by the touchstone of the commonsense surrounding him.

And to these we may add the rule of primitive obedience, to which reference has already been slightly made:

(4) Expect the child to recognize the existence of a moral law limiting the exercise of his activity, and to accept the conditions thus imposed with perfect obedience.

Obedience of a higher kind is derived from the co-operation of the first three conditions with the fourth, or rather a development of them to meet it; but the rougher primitive virtue cannot be dispensed with throughout life, and is invaluable in the early stage as setting a limit up to willing conformity, with which it is a natural object of the will to develop. The mistake that used to be common about the virtue of primitive obedience was that of overworking it in the most shameless manner, making it do duty for all other virtues to the great detriment of them and it. The common error now is to ignore its importance altogether; and this is a cruel training for adult life in which the rigour of limiting conditions has to be endured with content.

So much for the beginnings of moral life and character, the water-courses which contribute their streams to its flood. Let us turn now from consideration of the form of character to its matter—the *content* of the ideas which govern life when well governed—, and to the function of education in supplying that matter.

Suppose a child *idealistic, vigorous willed, susceptible, obedient*—using each word in the sense of our four rules. Suppose such a one face to face with the conditions of life in an ordinary well regulated home. What will he do? He will find—(I said a well regulated home)—that he is expected to do, and to abstain from doing, a number of actions, but that considerable freedom is allowed him in details and during his time of play. Some of these duties he takes as a matter of course; some of them he enjoys; some he dislikes, but is obedient. If he be, indeed, of the high-spirited sort, he is never readily obedient to what he *continues* to dislike. In that case he either rebels or learns to like it; and the latter is an easier task to him than it is to act without the sense of his own initiative behind the act. But in either case he accepts his social and physical world, and *thinks* himself more or less into his *necessary* place of an agent in it.

There is, however, a voluntary place also for him which he can make if he will. He has much freedom—room to develop his active impulses and the emotions implied in them; and he has the human ability to forecast, little by little, his life by thought. Into what place in his little social system will he feel and think his way? Upon the use he makes of his freedom, much more than upon the promptitude of his obedience to necessity, does his moral future depend.

Here appears the distinction between the selfish and the social nature, between the mind whose practical ideas are inspired by personal desires, and the mind under the lead of the affections, or of interests not centering in self. Either through the affections, or through interest in ideas to be fulfilled, the social nature develops itself and defends the mind from absorption in purely selfish aims. "If he begins to calculate," says Herbart, "he is lost to pure morality," the calculation being understood to apply to considerations of personal gain by means of personal actions. The expression may be too strong, but it must be admitted that if a little child begins to calculate on the rewards of goodness to any large extent, in cases where the promptings of affection would be more natural, it does not augur well for the future of that child. The calculation of interests to be served has its proper place in morality, but this is not its place. *Calculation of interests should not take place until interest has been so widened* as to include the whole of that object, the service of which may, in these later stages, be conceived as the object of morality.

Development of interest—many-sided interest—interest in all that goes on about him—this is the condition that the rightly-valued freedom of the child should be rightly used. Through widened interest the individual is changed and widened, till his will is brought into living touch with the will of the community surrounding him, and its good becomes his.

In this, education may play a most effective part. Interest is a matter both of feeling and of knowledge. The quickening of sympathy brings the mind of the child into harmony with the feelings, and to perception of the needs, of others; and thus a whole range of interests—the special social interests—is established. Affection emphasizes this effect, and by the depths of possible self-devotion which it reveals strengthens and deepens the social nature. Every good home educates much in this strain, and the strain of sympathy should run through all educational, as through all social, relations. It quickens the mind to its work by drawing it away from that obstinate absorption in self and self's discomforts, which is the great obstruction to progress in objective interests of all kinds.

An interest in the ideas, intentions, purposes of others is quite as essential as interest in their feelings and needs; and this interest once established leads readily on to interest in abstract ideas of social welfare, of scientific progress, of the reformer's hopes and the statesman's plans. In their measure, according to their understanding of it, children can be in touch with all the living social ideas around them. The parent should, as it were, take the child by the hand and lead him to the place whence he can see how full of life and work and hope and courage this great world is, that the child's mind may go out to it with wonder and interest and the aspiration that he too one day shall play his part in it.

And no less in small things than in great things should interest be cultivated. Kindness to animals, interest in natural objects, curiosity about the wonders of science and art—these are all elements in an individuality well compounded for a happy and useful life. A vast multiplicity of interests takes for the well educated man the place of a narrow round of desire for the boor. Thus there is always something of interest to see, hear, or do, and interests of these sorts are seldom of an anti-social character.

The mind of a child thus trained to act freely in accordance with social interests will naturally form, or tend to form, some idea of a plan of life for self. Some honourable ambition early formed, even though it be changed later, is a part of the normal process of the good life. It belongs to the dignity of man that he should have an aim

—not drift contentedly in the mere enjoyment of life from day to day. Parent and teacher can forward the formation of some purpose, temporary or permanent, and it would be well that the purpose should be of such a kind as to require some effort for its attainment in the present. The barren dream of good is a great danger. The mind may get into the habit of living *on* instead of *by* its ideas. The well trained child has some purpose, small or great, which he is fulfilling *now*.

Reference to purpose makes further progress more easy. The value of *persistence* in plans becomes obvious to the child himself when he has a purpose behind the plans. Training to persistence in a task, and faithfulness to promises, forms a most important element in moral training. We all know the child who begins several pieces of work at once, and finishes none of them. This is very bad, and must not be allowed to continue. Either by showing displeasure, or by convincing of waste and wrong, or by simple compulsion, if all else fails, the lesson must be taught that tasks begun should be finished, that the unfinished task voluntarily begun is a disgrace to the beginner.

The sacredness of a promise is another lesson for which there is need and occasion in the everyday life of the home. The sense of this sacredness goes with the sense of manly dignity implied in faithful persistence of purposes; and it introduces, on the other hand, that tender regard to the expectations of others on which depend so many of the finer shades of moral character. Closely bound up with this is the obligation to truth and sincerity in all things, the lessons on which are probably best driven home by the same double-headed hammer, appeal to manly dignity and to social sense. I think a lie looks at its worst to a child when it shows the liar as an object worthy of self-contempt; but the reminder that a liar's word is useless, and that no one believes what he says, is no less of value in training.

Without attempting to run through a whole catalogue of the virtues, I feel that a word is due, as regards general training, apart from instruction, to the fundamental virtues of courage and self-denial. The easy lives of a well protected, highly civilized generation render these virtues difficult of cultivation in childhood now. At least, it is somewhat easy to neglect them, and it does not do to let them take their chance. The educator, therefore, must secure opportunities as they occur, and, if necessary, make them.

Into each life should enter, and early enough to mould it, some hard fare, some hard living, something to do without, something to bear. It is useless to sing songs and read stories about courage and self-denial, and revel in luxury all the while. If self-denial is to be learned it must be practised, as our forefathers very well knew. There are causes enough for which children can be encouraged to give up something, and care should be taken that the act is the child's own, done by his freedom, not of necessity. This will be well, but I doubt that it is enough if the general level of life is full of ease and luxury. Moral fibre is sure to suffer if the tastes of childhood are formed on too high a standard of comfort. At least we should so order their lives as to ensure to them the capacity of dispensing with it for the sake of higher aims, should the need arise.

Practice in courage is still harder to get. Fortunately the race has inherited a large stock of this essential from earlier generations. Still there is a dangerous tendency at times to despise it as a mere physical quality—as if the muscles of the body were to despise the bones and sinew for not being muscle. And there are probably a good many men in our town population who would not be at all astonished to find themselves in full flight at the first sight of an enemy. Yet it is a primitive and for ever fundamental quality of the man who lives his life well that he should be able to stand steadfastly at his post in spite of danger. We do well, therefore, to encourage all those instincts in youth, which invite to manly sports and adventurous enterprise in which it is possible to be hurt, and especially those in which safety depends on courage, presence of mind, and skill in the face of danger.

In a later chapter we will deal with the system of virtues in more detail. An adequate conception of that system is necessary to all who have to do either with direct moral instruction or with moral education of the practical kind. But enough has been said to indicate in a preliminary sense the general nature of moral practice.

The purpose of the chapters which follow is to discuss the problem of direct instruction in morality. On the practical solution of this problem in each case depends the efficiency of all lessons—regular or incidental —that may be given on life and conduct, by the parent in the family, the teacher in the school, and the preacher speaking in church or assembly. In all such lessons it is intended that the attention shall be arrested, the intellect employed, the appropriate instincts and sentiments evoked, so that the thought and purpose of the learner may build itself up within him in accordance with an ideal of well-being and well-doing to which his conduct *ought* to conform.

Are there any who have doubts as to the usefulness *for* morality of such lessons *in* morality? Such doubts are strange; but they exist. They exist as the form taken by a revulsion of feeling against those faulty methods of instruction in all subjects from which the more scientific spirit of our age is gradually emancipating the whole field of education, and the evils of which are the greater in proportion to the importance of the subject. Mr. Squeers, no doubt, taught arithmetic so as to deaden to the utmost his pupils' minds. One may well rejoice that Mr. Squeers did not give systematic lessons in morals. Example is certainly better than precept, when the example is good and the precept unintelligible. Apart from Mr. Squeers, it may be said that a generation which taught its little stock of scientific truth unscientifically—that is dogmatically—was not likely to teach morality as a living doctrine. Mere verbal statements, made and heard as such, do not constitute real teaching in any subject. To learn "by heart" either Euclid's propositions or "My duty to my neighbour" is to acquire deadness of intellect where life is essential. Such a stupefying process stands, in all its forms, condemned.

But real teaching is a very different thing. It aims at the development of the mind in relation to the subject matter. Its object is complex, its methods subtle and highly skilled; but as to the value of the achievement there can be no doubt. He who makes another think has not lived in vain; and surely among all achievements of instruction none can outweigh that by which the growing mind is led to think and feel its way towards an ideal of life with which it can, in all the fulness of its powers, be satisfied.

To succeed in such an attempt it is not enough to study—though we shall make it our business to study—the ideal to be taught. We must study also those movements of intelligence and instinct which are involved in the successful learning of that ideal. And to this study let us now proceed.

CHAPTER I.

THE INTELLECTUAL PROCESSES INVOLVED IN THE STUDY OF MORALITY.

OUR first business is to distinguish instruction in morality from the wider problem of moral education, of which it forms a part. Moral education is concerned with the whole of the process by which persons grow from worse to better, and with the external conditions favourable to that growth. A full account of it would show in detail the inner working of all the leanings that "make for righteousness," and trace the relation of these to all circumstances in the environment which either help or hinder them. Among those inner founts of energy that make for good is the well-informed and soundly working intellect that knows how to discriminate evil from good; and the *problem of moral instruction is this—How can we by working on the intellect of another determine the whole nature of that other in the direction of righteousness?* Thus it comprises two questions: (1) How can the teacher *control and stimulate the ideas* of the learner to take certain forms? (2) How can he do this so that those ideas shall *not be mere ideas* barren of all product except more ideas—shall be fraught with motive urgency in the regulation of conduct?

All attempts at instruction in morality imply a belief in the existence of answers to these two questions; and thereby they imply an opinion that ideas do influence life and can regenerate character, and that instruction can influence ideas. But to believe these two statements simply is to grasp only half the truth. They are true, but true conditionally, and to know the conditions in any particular case is to be able to solve the problem in that case.

Persons have noble ideas of life and character, and yet do not act upon them. And ideas are poured out day after day in every school in Europe, without any result on the ideas of the child. In the latter case, this happens because the conditions of instruction in general have not been realized, and the *teaching* is bad. In the former case, since the ideas are moral ideas and ought not therefore to exist without being effective, we may say with equal emphasis that they have been wrongly *learned* : there was something wanting or wrong in the conditions under which they were acquired, in consequence of which they were created to be barren.

It will be our business, therefore, to consider :

(*a*) The conditions that are fulfilled in all successful instruction whatever the subject matter ;

(*b*) The conditions that are fulfilled in the production and maintenance of ideas of conduct when they really work as practical ideas.

Behind, however, there lies a further question as to the general intellectual conditions of moral progress. To quicken the operation of these conditions is better than to impress ready-made ideas. Let us begin, therefore, by considering how intellect works in relation to the moral life. In what ways does reflection tend to regulate conduct and develop character?

We may broadly distinguish two ways at the outset. (1) Good character grows by the *practice* of right conduct, and *ideas of right conduct* tend to produce the practice, and are themselves produced directly by a process of imagination and reason. (2) Good character grows by constant attention to *right ideas of character* on all occasions of action and deliberation.

These ideas constitute conscience, or the moral standard in its subjective and most familiar aspect. Character itself grows about and clings to them, and they control conduct more or less effectively, even before they have brought character into subjection. Such are the ideas of truth, honour, purity that go to make up our idea of a satisfactory self.

There are therefore two obvious methods of moral training intellectually considered; and both are necessary. The first is to train the learner to *think* about conduct, in order that he may form for himself a *reasonable* scheme of conduct—reasonable in the complete sense of being a scheme which must recommend itself to every one in so far as he thinks it out—a scheme that can be recognized as good universally—a scheme, therefore, which is instinct with regard for the feelings and thoughts of others. The second is to train him so to think about character, and with so much imaginative garniture and emotional colour, as to bring to the supreme place in *self*-consciousness an ideal of self consistent with this scheme of conduct.

The first is the more obvious, safer, and easier method, and the second cannot be separated from it as a matter of educational practice. But different minds work differently under the same procedure, and the teacher needs to keep this fact in view, else by labouring one aspect of a lesson too much he may lose his hold on those learners who more readily attach themselves to the other. Every lesson on conduct implies a lesson on character—on a sort of person; and neither should be neglected. The lesson on character goes home of its own accord when the self-consciousness of the learner, as one who acts out what he is, awakens to appropriate the idea of that sort of person. The wise teacher makes this happen: the child feels that he would like to act and *to feel himself acting* like, for example, the brave heroes of Thermopylae in Grecian story—to feel himself like one of them.

The emotional glow which accompanies this idea of self as so and so, transmutes the bare idea into a practical aspiration to do likewise; and if an opportunity occurs to express this, and it is expressed, in conduct, a complete step is taken in the establishment of a working ideal of character. It is important that the emotional glow should occur; but it cannot be forced. The teacher can see that there is opportunity, and time, and the stimulus of sympathy in his own feeling: the rest is by the grace of human nature working in the individual mind. So far as deliberate plan goes, the purpose to be kept in view is, therefore, mainly the development of a rational ideal of conduct, the reference to self as agent not being neglected.

Let us turn, therefore, to consider in detail the intellectual processes concerned in the creation of this rational ideal of conduct, and the conditions under which they work efficiently to that end.

That imagination plays a large part in this, as in the production of all practical ideas, every one will suspect even before inquiry. Imagination, indeed, plays a large part in all mental activity. By frequent excursion into the concrete realities it saves thought from becoming mechanical. In this case it more specially concerns us in two aspects.

(1) Dramatic imagination is imagination of

consequences dealing with the development of events. It is an exercise of dramatic imagination when the idea of a particular event bodies itself forth in a series of more or less concrete images of other events that follow from it in the logic of natural consequences. The minds of the masters of history, drama, and romance work in this way. The matter of history, for instance, is thrown into the form of natural sequence: on this side of it the process is logical, and could be performed by the scientific or specially rational mind but little prone to bodying forth its ideas in vivid imaginings. But the master of the art of narration does so body it forth: the events live and move for him in images more or less vivid; he sees and hears and feels the events as they march forward. So, under the pressure of imagination, he expresses himself in its terms, thus reaching the imagination of others and their reason through it. The merely rational writer of history is very good in his way: but every one will be aware of the difference between his pen and the pen of a writer like Macaulay whose touch appeals direct to the graphic imagination.[1]

Now it is evidently a means to moral guidance that a proposed course of conduct should suggest its series of probable objective consequences both good and evil. There can, of course, be too much of this, but there is more likely to be too little. These consequences may be suggested merely in the logical degree, that is, *not vividly*, and this is enough when the mind is already made up to its course of action relative to such consequences. For example, if I have settled it with myself as an ascertained fact that under certain circumstances pastry disagrees with me, it is sufficient for me to think of

[1] As between writers of novels differences in imaging power show themselves in various ways. The most noticeable defect is the failure of some to make the moderately well-endowed reader *see* the persons and scenes of the story. They are described, but not seen from the description, and it may happen that the visual imagination of the reader comes to be stirred rather by some side-issues in the story, and that he *sees* the heroine or hero persistently as different from the given description. In marshalling the march of historical events the graphic touch makes all the difference to the picturesqueness of the sequence.

this coldly, and not to imagine my possible sufferings, to secure abstention. But if my mind were not so made up, a touch of vivid concrete imagination would be necessary to produce the same effect, simply because the image has practical force which the logical idea has not. I take another example: Two boys go out to sea in a boat; a storm threatens, and they are ignorant and unskilful in the management of the boat. They are both equally aware of the probable consequences of persistence in their course—two consequences—(a) they will run great risk of being drowned, (b) they will give a great deal of trouble to the people on shore who attempt to save them. But the imaginative boy realizes all these possibilities as the mere thinking boy does not; they sting him with real anticipation of result and prompt to prudence. He feels, in imagination, the cold plunge when the waters engulf them, the futile efforts to hold the boat, the cruel slash of the waves, the wild attempts to make way: he sees the crowd on the beach, the gallant effort to rescue, the sorrowing group of relations and friends. But he does not need to go so far as this: one or two really bold images of consequent evil are sufficiently deterrent.

More definitely ethical cases will easily suggest themselves. I have said enough, however, I hope, to show what is meant by the claim that a certain *due* amount of dramatic imagination is an element of moral guidance, because it predisposes the mind to trace and realize the consequences of action. This realization tends to guide conduct from time to time in accordance with the rational ideal of conduct, and leads to the permanent establishment of that ideal in the individual mind.

But it may be objected that there is danger in an excess of this habit of mind, as likely to produce fearfulness, over-prudence, and other ills. This I at once admit, though it should be qualified by pointing out that such evils occur because the vividness of the imagination is out of proportion to its logical grasp—not because there is too much intensity strictly, but because there is too little extensity; and this leads to the further practical observation, that the cultivation of logical grasp is, of the two, more in the hands of the teacher, and more likely to be encouraged by deliberate training.

It behoves us, however, to remember the existence of the over-imaginative child, to learn how to detect him, and to modify our procedure in his case. English children are probably more likely to imagine too little than to imagine too much: the undramatic Teuton predominates over the dramatic Celt, and, therefore, for English children on an average, or treated *en masse*, the training of the imagination for effects is an important branch of education. All the more do we need to be careful for the few scattered lambs who have quite enough of it. The best thing for them is to keep their *thoughts*, in the logical sense, employed.

(2) We may distinguish the dramatic from the sympathetic imagination, closely connected

as these two uses of imagination doubtless are. The first is more directly under the guidance of logical thought, bodying forth a chain of consequences in vivid concrete terms. The latter comes into play under the stimulus of the sympathetic impulse to interpret the mind of another. This may be a very complex representative act, but in its general character it is of the nature of ordinary perception. The common object perceived—say a cow browsing on the mountain side—is in our perception of it a complex representation founded on the effort to interpret as signs a few sensory impressions. Similarly, when the signs present to observation are those indicating another person's state of mind, that state is perceived in the effort of imagination to interpret the signs by the production in the perceiving mind of a like state. When this effort is successful, the perception of one mind by its reflection in another is a perception of peculiar significance and intimacy, and well deserves the wonder and admiration so commonly bestowed upon it. Some minds are more gifted in this way than others, and all are limited as to the kinds of states in others which they can echo in themselves, so that even to the most gifted some persons will be unintelligible. All, however, can improve such gift as they have, as will be seen when we inquire into the conditions under which this response of mind to mind takes place.

In the normal case—the only one that directly concerns us here—the movement of imagination starts from the sympathetic impulse. The hungry little child crying in the street is not a mere sign of mental distress to be interpreted intellectually. The self in us is moved, by the signs of feeling, into harmony with the feeling signified. At first this fellow feeling may be very clumsy and wide of the mark; we are moved towards what we take to be the other's feeling, but we may mistake the signs of it as easily as we mistake objects too far off to be clearly seen. The sympathy of some persons never gets beyond this stage; they continue to mistake. This is partly because of natural slowness in accommodation of mind, so that, having responded at first with such feeling as came uppermost, they are not apt to move from that position. It may also be partly because of dulness in perception, so that they do not feel called upon to tune their feeling into the harmony of which it failed at the first. And it may be that, though naturally slow and dull, they could transcend these limitations by taking more pains to open their minds and correct their clumsy impulse, till the response became adequate to the feeling responded to.

Now the slowness with which the mind throws out new feelings to meet the case is correlative with slowness of imagination in forging the images corresponding; and the process of correction by which, slowly or swiftly, the one mind is tuned into harmony with another is largely, though not wholly, an intellectual process. The sympathetic movement detains attention on the signs of the other person's state of mind, and, at the same time, stimulates the *ideas* of self-consciousness, till some ideal construction is formed which fits all the signs and carries the true response of feeling with it. Thus, though sympathy belongs to the sphere of feeling, it not only acts as a stimulus to the imagination, directing it to certain ends, but is itself made perfect by the perfection with which imagination constructs out of the ideas of self-consciousness the required representations of states of mind. Thus we may speak of the sympathetic imagination, and note that the conditions favourable to it are :—(*a*) the sympathetic impulse, (*b*) facility of imagination in general, (*c*) richness, variety, and interest in self-conscious experience as the material of sympathetic imagination.

To the sympathetic impulse as such we will give further attention in another chapter. We are here concerned with the intellectual process of imagination—(*b*) and (*c*)—connected with it, and to this must be added the social tact which is readily observant of expression in persons, and thus corrects flightiness in social imagination.

When this social or sympathetic imagination is vigorous and true, the man goes on his way from day to day with a habitual other-consciousness as natural to him as his consciousness of self or of the natural objects about him. Conduct is largely controlled by this actual presence in our minds of the represented minds of others. The characteristic case in morals is the imagination of the consciousness of others as affected by our present conduct. We come in late when the household has gone to rest, and move about silently, checked by the fancy that some other person may be roused from sleep. Or we are careful to be punctual at an appointment, stimulated by the visual image of a friend waiting drearily in the rain. An imagined look of disappointment on a face will set us to do inconvenient things without any great occasion. And notice that the force of the stimulus lies largely in the vividness of the imagination, to which vividness the personal sting of motive seems to be proportional.

Many problems of conduct present themselves most aptly in these terms: How does the act correspond to the feelings, the wishes, the natural expectations of some other or others? As a sole guide to conduct, reliance on other-consciousness would sadly fail, but none the less does the imagination of it take its place, side by side with the imagination of consequences generally, as factors in the process by which a person is enabled to construct his act in accordance with a sound ideal of conduct. The dramatic imagination, with its long sight into the future, acts, moreover, as a safe check on a social imagination that may be short-sighted and look to the immediate future only.

Let us pause for a moment to consider the kind of person likely to result from the play of moralizing factors so far considered. It would be a person dominated by concrete imaginings of good and evil results, by vivid representations of other persons' desires, sometimes marvellously correct and to the purpose, but sometimes exaggerated and wide of the mark, and, above all, without a steadily realized criterion of moral judgment to enable distinction between mere fancy and the imagination of truth. Jane Austen delighted in drawing this bright and erring character in her somewhat over-abstract but very graphic way. The reader will be reminded in particular of Emma, her fancy always busy with romantic schemes for other persons' happiness, her sympathies for ever engaged with feelings in others which did not exist. And the reasonable Mr. Knightley, with his sound judgment and strong sense, is always ready to reprove and to point out the defect. "She will never submit to anything requiring patience and industry and a *subjection of the fancy to the understanding.*" Emma, however, is rather an example of unbridled fancy than of fancy combined with strong, even if unguided, sympathy. A quick perceiving sympathy is in itself a guide, because it leads fancy in definite ways having some rough accordance with the actual condition of things. Even sympathy, however, true though it may be to the immediate circumstances as affecting others, will run riot and give confused directions if not under the control of thought. It is on the *labour of thought* that *self-consistency* in imagination and conduct depends. He who will not take the trouble to think is like the double-minded man described by the apostle, "unstable in all his ways"; he is "like the surge of the sea driven by the wind and tossed."

Imagination, dramatic and sympathetic, as we have been considering it, does indeed imply no small amount of real thinking at its back. But enough thinking will hardly be brought into play in ethical instruction if distinct and separate attention is not given to the function of thought as such. Whatever the subject matter of the lesson may be, the lesson is not a good one if it does not bring the *judgment* of the learners into play, and lead them to use the *idea* conveyed in it as one more brick in the erection of a rational ideal of conduct destined to dominate as a permanent purpose the whole course of life.

An ideal of conduct is a highly complex practical idea summing up all the ideas of conduct already acquired in particular cases. If these ideas contradict each other, either one blots out the others simply, or the whole in which they are comprehended is shaken to its fall: some propping up or reconstruction is necessary, the characteristic of which is that it must secure freedom from contradiction in the new whole. An idea containing glaring contradictions breaks at once: an idea containing feeble contradictions that occasionally suggest themselves is in perpetual flux. The idea is not in equilibrium unless its contradictions are either settled or expelled: then it is at peace with itself and stands. But it is always liable to disturbance from without by the advent of new ideas claiming a place in it, and their admission may break up the idea or may be the occasion of fresh reconstructions. A stable idea is one that is sure to reconstruct itself after disturbance, and obviously that must be because it already contains so much truth that it cannot be essentially changed by any further discoveries.

A rational ideal of conduct is one stable in this sense: it does not contain all practical wisdom, and may contain some error, but the wisdom prevails so much over the error that all future access of wisdom will not destroy the whole but develop it. Such access of wisdom comes by the activity of intellect already considered, acting in contact with experience and opinion. Error also comes that way, but the stable idea—stable because mostly true—easily expels error. No possible access of error can be so large as to upset an ideal of life which is firmly rooted in everlasting principles of reason. Such access of error will cause particular errors in conduct only till found out as error by its inconsistency with that ideal to which the will has attached itself. In an interval of sophistication the man whose conscience is in general broad-based and true may lose his bearings for a time, like mariners in a fog, but he will soon recover his course by recurring to the sure chart and compass within him. And just as error is easily expelled, being an alien substance, so is the new wisdom which is cognate to the established ideal as easily received. Thus the rational ideal grows steadily towards completion: it has, like the mariner's use of chart and compass, a unity throughout time, as well as the unity of its present self-consistency at any time.

For instance, compare the moral future of two children, one of whom has been trained throughout to form his life in accordance with the universal principles of "justice, mercy, and truth," while the other has been guided through childhood by considerations of aesthetic fitness, good form, and conventional propriety. The difference is made by appealing, on all occasions of appeal, to a different range of motives in the two cases.

The one child grows up to view his life in all particulars with a steady regard to the reasonable claims of others, and to the maintenance of his own personality in the strict consistency of reason. Against principles of life so universal in their application, impulse may fight and win, but error has no chance. The man so built is not tempted, for instance, by specious arguments showing that pleasure is man's natural end and each one's pleasure for himself. On the contrary, the tempter who appeals to his intellect almost certainly loses him by wakening the ideal of rational life. His temptation comes rather in the day when thought is torpid and impulse strong.

But the other child has no clear view of universal principles—no firm grip on them as principles of life. He is governed by an ideal of good taste, and the ideal may be very complete in its way and effective too for good so long as it is not disturbed by new ideas. The man is trained to be a "gentleman" well balanced in his instincts, polished in his manner, and agreeable in the aesthetic sense to other persons. The appeal to motives for conduct in him has proceeded on this aesthetic plane. He is a charming person, and may live a life well ordered and beneficent. Balance, and polish, and an eye to the fitness of things, are all good—even very good—and moral training should take account of them. But they do not form a sound ideal of life: all their maxims are of *particular* application; exceptions may be made to them, and therefore they may be attacked. Matters of taste are in their nature liable to be disputed. Thus, on a moral ideal rooted solely in good taste, occasional error is sure to make profound and destructive impressions. Thus, when the man goes wrong under the lead of impulse, it is more likely than not that he will, by argument, bring his ideal of life down to his real level. And under social influence, or low-toned literature, or contact with moral scepticism in any shape, such an ideal is likely enough to break up as a moral ideal altogether, even in the absence of strong impulsive temptations. Thus it exemplifies the quality of instability.

The stable moral ideal is stable because, although perhaps including several non-essential or contingent elements, it is for the most part based on universal truth. Thus it is for the most part in agreement with any total ideal of conduct that the human mind is capable of forming. It disagrees with many ideas on the subject—might even disagree with the majority, each in its isolation voting "No." Truth may never have a majority in her favour, because every error cries out against her. But she is the diverging point of all error none the less. The many errors distribute themselves about the one truth, and mark her place as the centre of their cluster.

Experience of life, and the imagination of such experience, supply the means for the development of new partial ideas in the total ideal of conduct; but the constant exercise of reflection and judgment is necessary, in order that the means should serve the end, and any permanent result be thus secured. Moral instruction, therefore, includes training to regular thought on the subject matter of conduct. Each learner in his sphere—in his degree—should be a moral philosopher, judging about cases of conduct, enlarging, establishing, his ideas of right.

Our reflections on the conditions of stability in the moral ideal will have brought to light an important educational precaution, the neglect of which is doubtless the cause of much moral ruin in later life. In any particular mind the stability of the ideal of conduct depends on its general conformity to the sum of the partial moral ideas likely to be suggested later. If then the ideal centres in a set of ideas of conduct likely to be contradicted in later life, so that these overbalance the more certain and indisputable part of its content, there is danger that the ideal as a whole may be overset for a time and even permanently shaken. It is unstable, and every blast of counter-doctrine will drive it farther from its moorings, because controvertible doctrine prevails in it over incontrovertible truth. This happens when persons have been taught to attach more importance to conventional non-essentials than to the broad requirements of charity, self-denial, and truth.

A similar result shows itself in an even more striking light as affecting the religious idea. Quite apart from the particular development of religious thought in which a man is brought up, the religious idea is stable in one, unstable in another. And why? Simply because the one has so learned the idea as to attach all its significance to the not easily shaken essentials, while the other has perhaps centred himself in the Scotchness of Scotch sabbaths or something equally inviting debate.

Good moral teaching presupposes in the teacher a rational ideal of conduct in his own mind—not by any means necessarily *the* complete rational ideal, but *a* rational ideal, one that begins at the right end so as to secure perfect stability. The teacher moreover must be able to teach—that is, to secure the exercise of imagination and thought in the ways that have been described—so that appreciation of conduct and aspiration for character may be present in the consideration of every particular case, while reflection surely and steadily gathers up the moral of every incident, to incorporate it into the ideal of conduct that dominates all good life.

This ideal, whether rational or irrational, complete or incomplete, is known to us under the name of conscience, controlling by encouragement or discouragement all our individual ideas of action. In the conscientious mind it is ever present—ready to permit or to forbid—as a permanent condition which all actions must satisfy. There are two ways in which conscience may fail, and good education should prevent either of these failures. It may fail to be present when required, and it may fail to dominate other motives even when present.

A habit of due deliberation in act is the

preventive of the first evil—an obviously effective one. We may deliberate too much, and we ought not to deliberate always, but to deliberate in doubtful cases is well. Impulse acts at once, conscience generally, though not always, takes time; for impulsive moral motives must be distinguished from conscience as a whole although they pertain to it.

The second evil is prevented by a habit of never-failing obedience. A breach of habit is much more than the negative evil of loss of exercise: it is the foundation of a positive habit of breach. Such a thing as a breach with conscience ought to seem impossible to the well-trained mind. The realization of its possibility weakens resistance to temptation for the future.

CHAPTER II.

THE MORALIZING INSTINCTS DEVELOPED BY THE STUDY OF MORALITY.

WE have seen how the activity of the learner's intellect is involved in any successful course of moral instruction. By such instruction he is trained to employ his powers of reason and imagination on every problem of life and conduct. Thus his moral consciousness is developed on the intellectual side. He comes to see his life as a consistent whole, harmonious with the lives of all his fellows, in so far as he and they do set their purposes on the ends that ought to be realized.

But in good instruction of all kinds, and in moral instruction more especially, there is at least as much training of the instinctive as of the conscious self. Not that a line can be drawn between these two branches of training, for in every movement of the mind towards its object there is an instinctive, as well as a conscious or ideal, source of energy. The ideal source we can explain in the reasons we give for the act, but it may well be that the energy of the movement chiefly depends on some instinct that hides itself in the silence of unconsciousness. These silent instincts are only known in their effects: they predetermine the flow of feeling, the direction of attention; and thus the train of ideas being biassed by them more or less, the whole mental life is subjected to an inner shaping force of which consciousness gives no *direct* account. Such shaping instincts make up, in the first instance, the original character —be it of "original sin" or of original righteousness. By directing the attention they determine even the course of our thought, and move us, moreover, to outbursts of feeling and action in which thought plays a vanishing part.

But the shaping instincts can themselves

be shaped: the development of character in adaptation to circumstances, or to the ideal of character, is such a shaping. It is this second kind of shaping that concerns us in direct moral instruction. Although the train of ideas is biassed by the original instincts, the ideas once present have an independent and powerful efficiency: they gather force by drawing in the whole intellectual reaction, and express themselves in conduct even as against strong opposing instincts. This is what we call self-control; and by practice in doing what we *see* rather than what we are impelled to do, a habit of self-control is formed, so strong that at last the opposing instincts cease to make their opposition felt, and in the long run the group of them is changed—old instincts have withered, new instincts grown up. Thus the fiery-tempered boy becomes by his self-discipline the gentle natured man.[1] And note that in his exercise of self-control he helps himself by

---

[1] George Macdonald's story, *The Marquis of Lossie*, finely illustrates this change.

calling largely on his sympathetic impulses and his intellectual perception of justice.

Self-discipline, this re-shaping of the instinctive self, has to be *worked out* in actual life. None the less is it true, however, that if it be true *self*-discipline it takes its rise in moral ideals firmly grasped. The source of the new life is the new thought—the "Word of life"—the ideal of a better self which, when clearly seen and steadfastly applied, is not too strongly described by the New Testament as a new birth. Hence it is the function of moral instruction to initiate, and re-initiate, and continually stimulate the discipline of self, into accordance with the moral ideal.

Our study of the intellectual processes involved in the learner's response to the teaching of morality will suffice to show all that is involved in the building up of the moral ideal as such. But the efficiency of the ideal for the self-discipline required involves other conditions than those of its own richness and energy intellectually considered; although it must be remembered that an idea into which is outpoured all those powers of thought and imagination already considered is an idea strong with the force thus gathered to express itself in life. One mind differs, however, greatly from another in respect of the practical efficiency of its ideas. This may be, in the main, a difference either in imagination or in elasticity of instinct. And so, whereas it may be sufficient with one to secure that the right idea has been acquired, another will require the assistance of auxiliary instincts supporting it. Thus, to refer once more to the passionate-tempered boy, the idea of reasonable conduct may not be strong enough or quick enough to check the outburst by itself, in which case the auxiliary instinct of *immediate* sympathy is the obvious desideratum. Suppose the first blow draws blood, the sympathetic impulse may spring out instantly; and even before the blow takes place this may, with imagination of hurt, avert it.

The instincts that are in general serviceable to the moral ideal may be called the moralizing instincts. They divide themselves into two groups—the personal and the social. The latter, which centre in the sympathetic impulse, are the more obvious in their usefulness, but as their development turns much on that of the personal group we will consider the latter first.

The most *de*moralizing instincts are some of those that have regard to self. These are—a most important and, within due limits, necessary group—all that make for the pleasures that *may* be used either (*a*) to excess, or (*b*) to the hurt of others. In a well-balanced character there is set over against these, with the effect to limit them, not only reason, but instincts that control them silently. Excess of every kind excites disgust in a well-constituted person: either the appetites are themselves limited, or a controlling instinct directed to this end of moderation holds the reins. No doubt, the mere physical appetites have this natural limitation in healthy physical natures; but the effect of moderation is produced over so vast a range of desires so far removed from our primitive wants, that a general instinct forbidding loss of balance and restoring self-possession is forcibly suggested. This is the instinct by which is maintained the normal humanity of the man—that due proportion and harmony of function which is threatened by particular exaggerations of every kind. When drawn by any such, the rest of his nature asserts itself in opposition to maintain the whole. The experience, I imagine, is a tolerably familiar one—that sense of strong though vague protest in us somewhere against our own even harmless extremes. The waters of consciousness are troubled by the stirrings of some instinct, which let us call the *instinct to self-possession*. This is a moralizing instinct: we appeal to it, as well as to reason, when we reprove a child for having "forgotten himself." In moral instruction it is appealed to frequently, in every appeal to the sense of dignified self-assertion that backs the moral idea of a well-balanced self. In a hundred ways may be said what Shakespeare finely says:

> "To thine own self be true,
> And it will follow as the night the day
> Thou canst not then be false to any man."

Against the *excess* of all natural desire there is the reaction of this healthy instinct to preserve the balance of self. Primarily it sets itself against *any* strong disturbance, and is not always a moralizing force. But it is capable of fine uses for good, to keep life in close touch with the moral idea of a self living fitly. When such an idea of self is established, this self-possessing instinct shows itself as a fixed tendency to preserve the idea. This is stimulated in every thought of self-respect, in every act of self-control, in every reflection of self-reproach, in every resolve to be the moral self.

Good moral teaching will aim at the development of this instinct by well-chosen appeals to the ideas that stimulate it, whether unmixed ideas of morality or not: heroic tales of endurance, abstinence, of the essential wealth that consists in the fewness of wants, of human dignity as bound up with independence of circumstances—all teaching and preaching that appeals to the human soul to make itself strong—tend to draw out into constant practice the self-possessing instinct.

But moral teaching does more than this. It aims at the development of all this strength in a soul based on the moral ideal. And so the appeal should be associated throughout with the idea of the better self asserting itself as *the* self, to possess and rule for good all vagrant impulse and desire. Endurance, abstinence, self-control, dignity, become more truly noble in the nobility of their end.

The conclusion, however, on which it specially behoves us at this point to dwell is that in the moral lessons careful account shall be taken of the natural instinct to be or to do something having a wholeness and individuality of its own. There are repressive requirements in the moral ideal, but let us take care that we draw out the positive forces of the child's half-developed personality to deal with them. Something more than pure intellectual discipline is involved in the intellectual teaching of self-control.

The impulse to *be* some kind of person is capable of use as a moralizing impulse, though it may be badly directed. In good moral instruction it is, not only directed, but drawn out. The impulse to *do*—to achieve some end chosen by self—is a moralizing instinct also, and calls for the same sympathetic treatment. Of the intellectual impulse to *know*, the like remark may be made—has been made already.

Over against all these impulses of human life—of life as human—stand the host of those impulses which subserve the manifold desire to *have*. In their effects there is this marked contrast between desires to *be* and desires to *have*, that the former, in general, aim at a result by which the world is made more desirable for others, whereas the latter seek a share in goods, the share of which for others is thereby diminished. Hence it is to the undue exercise of these acquisitive desires that the vice of selfishness attaches. When the interests of another are not threatened or neglected there is no selfishness. It is not selfish, therefore, to desire much virtue and knowledge, but it is selfish to desire the lion's share of land and houses and material goods.

And this brings us back to the division we made in the subject of demoralizing instincts at the outset. Any instinct may be demoralizing which makes for the pleasures that may be used to the hurt of others. These form a large and immensely powerful group under the general ill-sounding name of Selfishness. Against these what instinct shall we rely upon to do battle for morality.

No part of the subject is more familiar than this part. A ready ally is found in the impulse of sympathy by which one man's state of mind is moved into unison with that of another. The importance of the development of sympathy, as a factor in moral education generally, has already been discussed at sufficient length. Here we need only dwell on its stimulation and direction in connection with the subject matter of the moral lesson. For instance, in a lesson where there is a story of tyrannical conduct, the child's mind goes out in revolt against the unmanliness of the tyrant's character, and also moves in a glow of sympathy with those whom he hurts.

In the course of moral lessons, sympathy is cultivated in relation to the imagination of other persons and their feelings. We have already seen how the value of the sympathetic impulse largely depends on the perfection of the imaginative skill which it is able to enlist in its service. It will be obvious, therefore, that the cultivation jointly of imagination and sympathy, which is so marked a feature of story telling to a moral end, is conducive in a high degree to moral culture. In real life, the sympathetic impulse, started by some familiar signs of weal or woe, takes the lead, and the imagination is stimulated to a progressive effort of interpretation. In a story or a lesson this order of development is reversed. In real life the danger is that imagination will not do its work, and sympathy fail in the perfection of its fit. In the story there is a very real danger that the real sympathetic impulse should not be stirred at all, in defect of that real presence of feeling which is its normal source. This is a danger to morality, because the habit of coldly imagining the mind of another, without any movement to repel or adopt it, contains capacities for cruelty which are obvious enough. There is need for care, therefore, in the reading of literature which stimulates greatly the social imagination, especially when the sympathy normally consequent on its stimulus is of the painful sort. Sympathy with pain is exhausting, even that modified sympathy which co-exists with the consciousness that the persons affected are all imaginary. It is the person of most active sympathy who turns from the tragic to the comic page; and we may be sure that the person who chooses to fill his imagination with the stuff that "penny dreadfuls" and the agony columns of the newspapers are made of, suffers no sympathetic response in self-consciousness to the pains of which he reads. In the common case of a taste for the literature of horror, it is likely that the activity of imagination is occupied almost entirely with the external facts—that the minds of the unhappy actors in the drama are not imagined at all. But undoubtedly there are cases in which the mind of the sufferer is imagined, though as a thing apart from self, evoking no response. Then we have cruelty, even if the suffering be only that of a hobgoblin in a fairy tale.

I would suggest, therefore, that the moral lesson should *aim* at evoking the sympathetic response whenever it appeals to the imagination with respect to the life of other persons. This is generally evoked by taking care that the *minds* of those concerned are included in the effort of imagination; thus the emotional nature will be roused as part and parcel with the intellectual reaction. Much more than this we cannot well do in the actual lesson, but we can remove impediments to the natural flow of feeling, and the stimulus of our own warmth will warm the colder souls to a quicker response. Moreover, something can be done to *shake the self-centring of the over-self-centred consciousness*, which is the chief drag on the natural out-goings of like to like in the emotional imitativeness of sympathy. All social life does this, and even in the nursery education of the little child there is abundant opportunity for the development of emotional interests outside self.

But if there be excess in the demand made on our sympathies—especially the painful sympathies—emotional exhaustion must be the consequence, accompanied probably by a self-defending effort to shut oneself off from the inordinate demand. This effort may be made in three different ways. We may shut our eyes altogether to the ills that distress us. In this spirit we pass over the columns in the daily paper headed "Indian Famine" or "Turkish Atrocities." Or we may go so far as to take in the situation logically—possibly with the view of deciding on the practical course that ought to be taken—and strictly restrain the imagination from giving it concrete form. Or, not imposing this restriction, we may give the matter our intellectual attention, may even realize the feeling of it to those directly concerned, and yet harden ourselves within ourselves, and thus not sympathize. Any of these methods of defence may be made habitual. They all, but especially the last, savour of callousness.

Thus there is evil in a course of moral lessons which overworks the sympathies. More especially the teacher should be sparing of pain. The more stimulating kind of sympathy should be preferred, such as that called upon in tales of heroism and loyal service in which there is a continual outflow of good deeds with increase of happiness from the hero's activity. When the deed of tragic heroism is used—and it ought to be used sometimes—it should have a sublime goodness sufficient to raise the mind rightly above considerations of pleasure and pain.

The sympathies should not be overworked, and least of all by way of exercise in moral lessons. Let care be taken also that their development does not terminate in mere sentiment. The achievement of some practical result by which things are improved should be the end of every sympathetic outburst. "Go thou and do likewise,"—this should be the unspoken moral of every lesson.

A true story of an Irish drummer-boy in Elizabethan times is told by Mr. Standish O'Grady, which so well illustrates the interaction of imagination, sympathy, and moral purpose, that I venture to quote it here. The drummer-boy marched with the army of the Queen under the Lord Deputy and Captain Thomas Lee, whose purpose it was to seize, in the dead of night, the fortress of a certain chieftain Clan-Ranal, otherwise called the Raven. The conversation between the leaders revealing their purpose is overheard by the drummer-boy marching near, who drops his drumsticks in the shock of his dismay.

"The drummer-boy drummed about as well as before that overheard conversation about the Raven had shaken the drumsticks from his hand. The sub-conscious musical soul in him enabled him to do that; but his thoughts were not in the music. Something then said caused to pass before him an irregular dioramic succession of mental scenes and pictures. For him, as he whirred with his little drumsticks, or rat-at-at-ated, memory and imagination on blank nothing for canvas, and with the rapidity of lightning, flung pictures by the hundred.

"Here is one for a sample: it passed before him like a flash, but passed many times. A long table, a very long table, spread for supper, redolent of supper, steaming with supper, and he very willing to sup. Vessels of silver, of gold too—for it was some gala night—shone in the light of many candles. Rows of happy faces were there, and one face eminent above all. There were candles in candlesticks of branching silver, or plain brass, or even fixed in jars and bottles. All the splendour was a good way off from him. He was at the wrong end of the long table, but he was there. At his end was no snow-white linen, and the cups and platters were only of ash or wild apple; but of good food there was plenty, and of ale, too, for such as were not children. It was the supper table of a great lord. The boy was at one end, and the great lord at the other; he was at one end and the Raven at the other. He was not kin to this great lord, whom he called Clan-Ranal, and to whom he was too young to do service. He knew no mother, and hardly remembered his father; he had been slain, they told him, 'when Clan-Ranal brake the battle on the Lord Deputy and all the Queen's host.'

"Again, in imagination, the drummer-boy sat in Clan-Ranal's glowing hall while the storm raged without and shook the clay-and-timber sides of that rude palace. There sat the swarthy chief, beaming goodwill and hospitality upon all. His smiles, and the flash of his kind eyes illuminated the hall from end to end, and made the food sweeter and the ale stronger. He was only a robber chief, but oh, so great! so glorious! in the child's eyes. His 'queen' was at his right hand, and around him his mighty men of valour, famous names, sung by many bards, names that struck terror afar through the lowlands. To the boy they were not quite earthly; he thought of them with the supernatural heroes of old time. He did not know that his 'king' was a robber, or, if he did, thought that robbery was but another name for celerity, boldness, and every form of warlike excellence, as in such primitive Homeric days it mostly is. To others, the Raven and his mighty men were sons of death and perdition; but their rapine sustained him, and in their dubious glory he rejoiced. A fair child's face, too, mingled always in these scenes and pictures, which chased each other across the mind of the drummer. He saw her, in short green kirtle and coat of cloth-of-gold, step down from the king's side at an assembly, bearing to him, the small but distinguished hurler of toy spears, the prize of excellence (it was only a clasp knife; he had it still), and saw her sweet smile as she said, 'Thou wilt do some great deed one day, O Raymond, Fitz Raymond, Fitz Pierce.' All the gay, bright happy life of his childhood, so happy because it held so much love, came and went in flashes before his gazing eyes; and now he drummed on the army which was to quench in blood, in horrors unspeakable and unthinkable, the light of that happy home where he had once been so happy himself. Tears ran down the drummer's face, unseen, for the night had now come. Then a thought, a purpose, flashed swiftly, like a meteor, across his mind, and came again less transiently, and then came to stay, fixed, clear, and determinate; a purpose like a star. He drummed better after that, and spoke as stoutly as his fellows about the glorious achievement which was to be performed that night, and about his share of the plunder. Yet his thoughts were not plunderous but heroic. He, Raymond, son of Raymond, son of Pierce, son of, &c., &c., would do a great deed that night. Some pride of birth may have mingled with the lad's purpose, for he was of a sept broken and scattered indeed, but once famous —the Fitz-Eustaces. He knew his genealogical line by heart. If there was a drummer at one end of it, there was an Earl at the other."

. . . .

"Then cautiously the Lord Deputy's army began to descend from the heights. Silence was enjoined on all, not to be broken on pain of death. Each subaltern was responsible for the behaviour of his own file; he had strict orders to keep his men together, and prevent straying on any pretext. As they drew nearer the scaling ladders were unpacked. The little city as yet gave no sign of alarm; not a cock crowed or dog barked. No watch had been set, or, if there had been, he slept. All within, man and beast, seemed plunged in profound slumber. Some strong detachments now separated from the main body, and moved through the trees to the right and the left. Their object was to surround the city, and cut off all retreat. There was another gate at the rear, opening upon a wooden bridge, which spanned a considerable stream. There were only two gates to the city, that in front, at which the main body was assembled, and the rear gate, whither the detachments were now tending. They never got there. At one moment there was silence, broken only by the murmuring of the stream or the occasional crackling of some trodden twig; at the next, the silence rang with the sharp, clear roll of a kettle-drum, the detonations so rapid that they seemed one continuous noise:

'Oh, listen, for the vale profound
Is overflowing with the sound.'

"As suddenly as that drum had sounded, so abruptly it ceased; someone struck the drummer-boy to the earth senseless, perhaps lifeless. But he had done his work. The roll of a kettle-drum can no more be recalled than the spoken word. The city, so sound asleep one minute past, was now awake and alive in every fibre."—*The Bog of Stars: by Standish O'Grady*.

So the chieftain and his household were saved, but forfeit was made of the drummer-boy's life.

CHAPTER III.

PRINCIPLES OF TEACHING.

WHATEVER the subject matter may be, the work of the teacher is in nine cases out of ten not done by directly enforcing the ideas he has in mind. To say what one has to say is so obvious a way of communicating information that if it be a wrong way the caution against relying upon it is doubly necessary. That it is not always a successful way every teacher by sad experience knows. It is only the brilliantly teachable few—the very very few—who take in, even temporarily, all the ideas that are poured out upon them. The teacher is therefore bound to inquire (1) what are the conditions fulfilled when a new idea is taken in, and (2) in what ways may the fulfilment of the conditions fail.

The first condition is that in some way or another it should *arrest the attention*. Attention is the first condition that the teacher has to secure, and there are many ways of securing it. The charm of personality—what the Americans call magnetism—is one way. Some persons are so delightful to look at, to hear, to watch, that they are always listened to, whatever they say. The ideas they express are at least attended to in the sense, and if not by the intellect, that is because they are not intelligible: sensory attention has been secured, but something equally essential is lacking. Now it is not possible to turn oneself into a person with this indefinable charm: it is a quality apt to be lost even by being reflected on. Those who have it tend to lose it, if they become conscious of their grace. But it is worth while to consider its nature, so far as to be able to avoid the external qualities that war against it—qualities that repel the attention of eye and ear. "Who wins the eye wins all," as the proverb says, and the same may be said of him who wins the ear. Hence the efficacy of attractive appearance, not necessarily beautiful, in face and figure and even dress, of graceful gesture, of musical voice, of eloquent speech, of all that engages and satisfies the higher senses and aesthetic feeling generally. Every improvement in these respects that the teacher can make in himself the better will be his grip on the sensory attention. But for some subtle reason it appears that beauty and appropriateness of movement and voice are infinitely more effective than mere good looks. The charm that gets a speaker listened to lies somewhere in these dynamic qualities. The positively disagreeable therefore in voice and movement should be cured, and the rest had best be left to nature. The art of good speech, however, *i.e. clear enunciation, true voice production,* and *good literary style* can be freely cultivated : these all tend to the right end—the arrest of attention.

There are ways in which the unsuccessful teacher contrives to repel this external but necessary attention. Affectation or its appearance, self-consciousness, over-emphasis, and all that is strained or laboured in manner, look, or speech—these repel, and much really good work may fail wholly of its effect in consequence. Oddities of most kinds first arrest attention, and then, when mere curiosity is satisfied, interest fails, and, finally, reaction sets in. There are, alas! people to whom one cannot listen.

The first, but only the first, step is secured when attention under aesthetic motives is arrested. A mere external attention is all that mere external attractivenes can permanently secure, if indeed it can secure even that as a permanence. A charming woman is sometimes watched and listened to with pleasure by one who takes no heed whatever of the ideas she expresses.

Attention that is not founded on an

intelligent interest in the subject matter has no permanence and little or no disciplinary worth. The teacher's first business is to secure this intelligent interest. He may have to lead up to it by a suitable preparation beforehand, or he may secure it by a sudden happy stroke. But for his choice of methods everything depends on the nature of the learner. The average disposition of the class should be his cue. Two cases of the modes in which interest originates may be broadly distinguished.

1. The most general case is that interest does not arise with respect to a perfectly new and unknown idea. The mind of the emptiest-headed learner is not a perfect blank. He busies himself with some ideas, be they ever so poor intellectually, or low in the moral order. Now, in defect of a highly-organized self-consciousness such as cannot be expected to exist in every one, it is rather in our particular ideas than in our minds as a whole that interest is excited. A lively idea on which the mind dwells

pretty often is easily aroused when suggestions bearing on it are either heard or read. It sustains and expands itself by entertaining these suggestions, and ultimately they are accepted or rejected according as they can or cannot be incorporated with the rest of the mental content. But whatever the final result in the workshop of thought, the first stage of interest depends on the fitness of the suggested idea to sustain and develop a thought already there. In practice it comes to this. Take any average group of young learners, and you will find that, for more than half the class, attention droops and interest flags unless you contrive so to deal with your subject as to be generally talking about something of which they are, or have been, thinking.

In moral instruction it is peculiarly easy to apply this truth. It is so easy and natural to found a lesson on some familiar incident which is in itself provocative of the children's thought—such as an unkind saying behind one's back—or to start the moral reflection arising out of some inspiring romance by bringing it to bear on everyday problems which have interest for all normal minds. Many children spend much unobtrusive thinking on questions of right and wrong that puzzle them. If the subject matter of a lesson meets such a question, then indeed is interest sure.

This cannot happen as often as it should if the children are not freely invited to take their part in determining the subject matter. Only the child himself knows about what he would take most interest in learning more, and the teacher leads best who follows with most skill, and yet to his own end, the lead of the child's mind. Freedom of inquiry is essential if interest is to be generally sustained. But this, of course, must not be allowed to degenerate into a Babel of disconnected questions. All learners cannot be expected to play the second part in dialogue so perfectly as Glaucon in the dialogues of Plato.

2. There are learners, however, who are

not so dependent on their particular old ideas for their interest in new ones. Some, like the Athenians of old, love always to hear, as well as to tell, some new thing. These are the essentially docile, about whom on this score no pains need be taken. Their intellectual vigour is so out of proportion to the occupations which claim it that they are ready to throw themselves into the appreciation of all presented ideas. This passion for miscellaneous appropriation decreases, it is true, as intellectual vigour finds more occupation in the ideas already present, but, to compensate this source of loss in docility, there is the gain due to increased range of intellectual interests as ideas increase.

It is a problem for the teacher how to make the most of such general docility as he finds. It is at this point that all his rhetorical arts come into play, all the arts that concern the composition and presentation of the subject matter so that it may be as interesting generally as it can be made to be. The requisites might be summed up under the heads of *close reasoning, transparence of expression,* and *literary beauty.* A well-sustained thought, clearly expressed in language that goes home to the intellect, is always attractive, and for many minds is more attractive than anything else. But add the charm of literary composition, elegance of form, and the variety in unity of well-arranged and aptly-illustrated subject matter, and the thought becomes irresistible if it be also intelligible : rational interest is sustained by the aesthetic motive.

For ethical lessons, these reflections point to the use of a good story, beautifully told, as the foundation of the lesson. If the teacher can *tell* the story well, so much the better; if not, it can be read. But for little children the actual telling counts for so much that some literary beauty can be fitly sacrificed for its sake. The moral purport of the story should be sooner or later made quite clear, and this is best done Socratically by a discussion with the class, each member bringing to bear upon it his experience and his inquiry for further light. But this leads to consideration of the *stimulus* to imagination which, in addition to the *arrest* of interest, all good teaching implies.

The good story may be listened to with attention, and the whole of the ethical lesson very much *enjoyed*, and it may yet fail to have the use intended if the mind of the child himself does not work upon it thoughtfully. As has been already indicated, many minds have a marked disinclination to attend, unless the ideas presented are wanted by them for further exercise of their own intellectual activity. In so far, therefore, as the lesson is calculated to gain their attention, it also secures the exercise on it of their imagination and thought. And this gives rise to the interesting and very consoling reflection, that it is better to interest a class by making its members all think, than to interest it by one's own rhetorical arts and skill. Great orators are often less permanently effective than would seem at first sight. It is not by the charm and impressiveness of one great speech that reforms are won, but by the stimulus to general thought which all great thinkers and good speakers at all times exercise. And this I call a consoling reflection, not because it is so easy to stimulate the imagination and thought of others, but because it is more possible, and more agreeable to the simplicity of human nature, to improve our gifts in this respect than to aim at the powers of effective oratory. No other expert is so little made and so much born to his vocation as the orator; and we are in our generation so aware of this fact that we scorn perhaps too much those rhetorical arts which it is our business to attain. The main art of the teacher, however, lies not in impressing the attention, but in stimulating the intellect.

The problem in every lesson is how to drive the idea home so that the *maximum of the intellectual work is done by the class*, that is, by each member individually. Each child is to be sent home with an idea, and his own mind working on that idea. If this does not occur, ideas in a sense may be impressed, but they are barren; and barrenness in a moral idea is a positive evil. Of a learner so taught it may be said, as some French writer says of women generally, that their ideas are stuck in their minds like pins in a pincushion. They do not form parts of a connected intellectual whole. There is not, therefore, any organic vitality in them, and so they are inoperative in regulating the scheme of life to noble ends. Many learners are so taught, and in other than moral subjects: the result is that their knowledge is no real part of themselves. It is impressed from without, not grafted on the living stock of freely springing thought.

To the extent required for this end, the teacher has to learn the very hard lesson of self-effacement. A managing, fluent-tongued, clear-headed teacher is often the worst teacher of all. He supplies all the ideas, does all the thinking, gets his set lessons well learned, and keeps his class in immaculate order. But his touch is like that of a dead hand. Intellectual life withers at his breath: initiative is checked, growth made impossible, except for the few who have vigour enough to rebel.

Now, it is not the positive energy and strength of such a teacher that is at fault, but their misapplication: these fine qualities are used to subordinate and check the minds of others, instead of being used more tenderly and thoughtfully, but no less vigorously, to stimulate these. It is never the positive qualities that are amiss, but the lack of some others that regulate properly their application. The naturally good teacher is vigorous *and sympathetic*. To such a one it is delightful to use his vigour in the increase of the mental life of another; and most persons are sympathetic enough to feel this if they give themselves a chance. The sympathetic thrill due to the sense of a dull mind quickening to life under one's touch is a pleasure of life not to be despised. A subject of such intimate human interest as ethics does not present serious difficulties in this respect. *Stimulus* is not difficult if its negative condition of *not* doing the learner's work for him be understood.

Imagination and thought are both stimulated when attention is secured in the way first described, by attaching the new idea to the original mental content for which it has a natural interest. The more perfect way of doing this—but it is not generally quite possible—is to make the learner choose the subject of his lesson. An approximation can be made to this, at least in the early stages where it is most desirable. The members of the class may be asked, either in rotation, or by some form of agreement among themselves, or by the teacher's selection of those who require most stimulus, to decide on the subject of the next lesson. "What shall we talk about next time?" The answer may be given in a great variety of ways — some particular incident, some moral quality, and so on. I cannot guess beforehand what form the inquiry might take. Some consensus of desire having been obtained, it becomes the teacher's business to find more material for the lesson in the interval, and to prepare a line of development in thinking out of the subject through which the learners are to make their way.

Under these circumstances, the imagination of at least those children who were interested in the choice of the subject will be very ready to work on any new, but cognate, ideas that either the teacher or their class-fellows may bring up. Two results are required, and it is easy to miss either. The learners have to imagine concrete developments of the subject—instances of courage for example—with all their essential detail and consequences. One child supplies such a case from experience, or the teacher does, and the others imagine it, opportunity in some measure being given to them to keep their imagination ahead of the narration and to forestall it, as one does in reading an interesting story. Judgment and reasoning are of course here involved, but it may be only as giving a lead to imagination and not as contributing to the proper work of thought.

But without this the lesson would be far from complete. One good thought is worth a hundred good fancies, so far as the permanent value of the lesson goes. The images of the fancy possess the mind one after another, and it is therefore possible for them to be inconsistent with each other. Courage may attract to-day, fear completely engross to-morrow. The image of the suffering poor may possess me one hour, the image of some pleasure project for myself the next. Under the control of the one image I am urged to give, but under the influence of the other I selfishly keep. Obviously a life under the influence of successive images has no unity; and the *psychological* characteristic of the moral life is that the idea of it is *the idea* that brings, or tends to bring, all practical ideas into unity. If, therefore, imagination be not controlled by the unity of thought, life is left equally open to the influence of all attractive fancies, whether good or bad.

It follows that there is a positive root of evil in any moral instruction that appeals merely to the imagination and has no stimulus for thought. This is perhaps the most common sin of the popular preacher. The result is a highly trained fancy very susceptible to *all* stimuli, and a character dangerously open to influences because quite without the habit of idealizing its impressions to the extent of bringing them into unity with one another. Such a person is inconsistent, unreliable, and, if trial comes in attractive guise, is sure to succumb. In common parlance we say, "He had good impulses, fine susceptibilities, but no principle."

If the idea of evil was intellectually as self-consistent as the idea of good, moral salvation by reason would not be possible;

but, so far is this from being the case, that it is obviously out of place to speak of *the idea* of evil at all: evil is in its nature plural, a whole of parts that strive with each other, and, in the mind, as in the world, strive more as evil increases.

It is not too much to say that all good teaching, which stimulates and trains to thought, is in its nature moral training. And so involved with sentiment and fancy is moral subject-matter, that it would not be well to depend for the whole of our training to moral reason on the thinking that can be got out of a moral lesson. But, with this word by the way for the ethical value of some discipline in a stiff intellectual subject, I return to the position that training to thought *on* the particular subject should be got out of every moral lesson itself.

The moral at the end of the tale is an idea or thought, so are the beautiful reflections scattered up and down, in the speech of the heroes and the self-communings of the author. If these ideas be impressed, they should be used as food for more thought on the child's own part. And, as before, the surest way to get his mind to work is to let *him* take the initiative in drawing rational conclusions so far as possible. At least he can be called on to supply the moral always, (since it comes at the end of the tale), and to be active in the discussion of principles to which every lesson should lead up. It is not true that children shrink from moralizing on their stories. Some do shrink from being *told* the moral in a pompous manner, but none shrink from drawing it for themselves. In this way they not only increase their store of moral ideas, but they train themselves for further increase from every story they read and from every event that occurs. As the lessons progress, the ideas increase and are brought into relation to each other, as parts of a scheme of conduct and character; and, this being done by their own thinking, the habit is ever more and more confirmed of looking at every event as having some moral bearings, some significance as to the righteousness of the conduct it calls for and implies.

Every good lesson culminates in this labour of thought which is performed separately as well as jointly by all members of the class. In this, however, the teacher has a power of determining beforehand—not only the end but—the course of development to the end, since, though all imagine differently, all, if they think correctly, think alike. Dealing with such subject-matter, some allowance must, indeed, be made for limitations of experience and for immaturity of power; but the unity, at the worst, predominates over the variety, and allows of a steady general march to the establishment of the ethical principle intended at first. To this end the teacher, at the last, takes definitely the command. There may be cases, however, in which it is wiser to leave matters in the end somewhat vague, when more thought is seen to be necessary.

Some considerations still remain. Philosophers and ordinary people alike have always doubted the truth of the view attributed to Socrates, that it is impossible for a man to have an idea of good conduct without acting upon it. Yet there is a sense in which this is true, a certain degree of vitality and energy in the idea which *necessarily* makes it operative on life. Not all ideas, though held with conviction, have this degree of life. Nor is it hard to see in what the difference psychologically consists. Activity of ideas is of two kinds: (*a*) There is pure ideation, or the activity of reason tending to wider generalizations and away from the concrete realization of the idea in images, practical or other. Ideas working ideationally keep their fringe of images in strict abeyance, and only use these for the purposes of thought. In a highly abstracted thinking mood there is absence of the train of images, and with that a suspension of contact with the external world, either to receive its impressions or to make impressions by acting on it. Ideas so working are not practical; and if they so work habitually, without emergence into imagination, they are not, as a rule, effective on conduct, because they do not flash out in images of acts to be done in the world.

Compare this with the activity of an idea that does flash out into images all along the line, while it is, or is not, being interwoven into the texture of abstract thought. Such an idea governs the images of fancy as they arise, prevents their emergence in act if contrary to it, and, through imagination, acts directly on the external world. The Idea of Good in Socrates' mind was no doubt of this kind, and an idea prone to work in this way is practical.

Now an idea of conduct ought to be practical, *i.e.* prone to influence conduct. Hence it follows that the ideas inculcated in the moral lessons must not be dealt with as pure ideational matter, like mathematics or a theory of chemical compounds. In avoiding the Scylla of unbridled imagination, we must steer clear of the Charybdis of mere abstract moral philosophizing. Human nature falls on this rock almost as naturally as on the other: hence the cold-heartedness of the moral pedant, the selfishness of the moral prig. Imagination has indeed to be kept in touch with reason, but reason must abut no less continually on imagination.

So the moral principles established in each lesson as ideas of conduct must be applied, at the time and afterwards, in imaginings of particular acts, and, best of all, outside the school-room, in the real acts themselves. Inside the school-room, however, the learners can apply themselves to picture forth what they would do under given circumstances. This practice goes farther towards a training to real conduct than is always admitted; though I admit at once that real conduct to the same effect is quite necessary.

A certain amount of emotional accompaniment seems to be favourable to the imaginative play of the central idea. Dry thought rushes on from thought to thought. To feel the charm of an idea is to pause over it, and by this pause it is established and made stationary for the time. But a thought is never idle: if not rushing on to weave itself with other thoughts, it sustains itself in images and acts. If not, it subsides. Thus the emotional thrill, the pause in thought, the flashing forth of appropriate images—all are aspects of the same process. Imagination is nearer to action than anything else but action itself, and emotional pause favours imagination.

If these pauses are desirable, how are we to bring them about. The first favouring circumstance is the beauty of the thought itself; and beauty occurs quite naturally in a thought, since it is thought that brings out its leading characteristic of variety in unity. The perception of this unity is the thought, and the emotional thrill and pause follows more naturally than not, except in exhausted conditions of nerve. Other persons — teachers for example — must *allow* the pause. It is not well to force it, or to try and work it up; but when several persons are together at the critical moment, sympathy accumulates the effect in each mind, and all are more apt to feel. Beauty of language is a great assistance, for every adjunct of beauty predisposes to the emotional pause, and the accompanying play of imagination. The labour of the idea is indeed retarded, but the emotional outburst in due measure is amply justified by establishing working images of the idea in character and in act. Nevertheless, emotional outburst, like imaginative play, must always be in due measure only, so that neither sentiment nor fancy may ever get the upper hand of reason, or in the long run retard her steady forward march.

But at every stage on that forward march the unity of reason naturally evokes anew the sentiment of beauty, and, through the pause of delight and the stimulus to imagination, life is once more brought into contact with reason and reason with life.

Of such a nature are the moral lessons that the best learners teach themselves in the course of their experience and reading. And this is the model for us, who venture, in all humility, to guide the self-teachings of youth.

CHAPTER IV.

THE SUBJECT MATTER. VIRTUOUS CHARACTER.

We come now to the consideration of a question that has engaged the thought of all good men, and the pens of all ethical writers since the world began. But we have to consider it from a point of view specially adapted to the educational purpose we have in hand. What is this rational ideal of conduct that the child is to learn, and in what order of development is it to present itself to him? This is a double question, but with a single answer. The rational ideal, intellectually considered, includes its order of development, and the accidental variations in it that will certainly occur are expressions of idiosyncrasy within that order.

The principle of this order is the principle of stability already discussed. The best order is that which, from the first, secures stability in the moral ideal. I do not say—far from it—that the moral nature as a whole grows necessarily in accordance with this order. The moral nature is not simply an emanation from the moral ideal. There may be much goodness with little idea of its nature. And, accordingly, moral education includes other factors besides moral instruction. A sound system of moral education is very wide and spreads a net abroad for all. And a sound system of training to moral thought is also diverse, and takes much account of individual habits of mind. But in the subject matter itself—the complex idea of character and conduct with which moral instruction deals—there is, *ceteris paribus*, a best order for its treatment, founded on consideration of the conditions on which maximum stability depends. A moral ideal uncontradicted at its centre from first to last, through all its developing complications, is a guarantee of moral certainty and strength. The core of it should be, if possible, such that neither experience, nor attractive opinion, nor the imaginings of romance will ever try to shake it. Temptations will assail it of course, but not the temptations of thought, or of fancy as controlled by thought.

The prime essentials of the moral ideal are the virtues that in all ages have been accounted such, the qualities that, in all poetry and romance, have been extolled as manly, dignified, and noble. The history of the human mind itself tells us what is most essential, and least assailable, in the idea of a life worthy to be lived. To live well means more to us than to our forefathers, but to them it meant, as to us it means, at least to live steadfastly—with dignity as becomes a man, with unity of purpose and with steadiness of aim. This is the irreducible minimum in the conception of a hero. Life can be *lived* confusedly, inconsistently, following the discordant lead of the instincts and the senses; but life cannot so be *thought* as a life worthy to be lived, or even permanently as a life worth living. An idea without unity falls to pieces, and is not an idea. Unity of purpose, therefore, and steadiness of aim are essential, not only to the idea of the good life, but to the very idea of a life that satisfies itself. And self-consciousness attaching itself to this idea is the sense of manliness or dignity. "This is my life, myself: this *I* intend to carry through: by it *I* stand or fall."

Here then is something more fundamental than morality, which is nevertheless so implied in all morality that character without it is a mere wisp of straw. We may fairly call this the *natural ideal* of life, since it is thus that a man must conceive of his life, if he conceives it at all in the strict sense as a consistent whole. The more a man thinks of his life the more must he think of it thus, as marching forward consistently and happily in pursuance of the ends he selects as good. Whether his final aim be power, or fame, or a dollar-pile, or social use, or domestic happiness, or a mixture of all these, he necessarily thinks of himself as pursuing it with steadiness and unity of aim. If he *imagines* himself otherwise, which is likely enough, it is either because he has not formed for himself any definite ideal of life, or he is aware, sooner or later, of the fact that his fancy has led him from his purpose, and he calls this weakness. The strong-willed man combats such weakness.

Now I believe that this natural ideal is more present in the minds of little children than we commonly suppose. When it is prominently present the child talks about what he means to do with his life, and his elders recognize the fact that this is a good sign. It is the best of signs: it shows the mind at work on an idea of life, and therefore amenable to the influence of cognate ideas. Too great definiteness, however, should not be encouraged, or encouraged with care; and discrimination needs to be observed lest the more backward in this matter of idealization should be forced beyond their pace. Children help each other best in this way: a few with ideals and purposes need little encouragement to set the minds of the others to work, till all have more or less caught the earnest tone.

The natural ideal is the *natural* core of the moral ideal, and, if at its core, is the best guarantee of its stability. The first lesson to learn from fairy tales and fables and stories of all kinds is that life has a purpose which each worthy life-bearer carries out consistently. This is the lesson which all heroic literature carries on its face. The hero lives to do something—to carry off the golden apples from the garden of Hesperides, to break through the circle of fire that surrounds the heroine, to avenge the death of his next of kin, to destroy the monster that devastates the neighbourhood, to pay the eric fine, or weregild, that the law has decreed; to guard the borders of his province single-handed from a multitude—he lives to do it, and he does it, or dies in seeking to accomplish it, faithful unto death. Purpose implies faithfulness to the purpose, and out of this core roll forth the heroic virtues one by one. In doing his deed the hero suffers loss and pain: even Jack the Giant Killer had some difficulties; and in all the best stories boldness and prowess are well balanced by the necessity of self-denial and fortitude. The allied virtues of patience, faith, and hope reveal themselves when the coming of success is delayed, and the highest point of the ideal is reached in the character of the hero made perfect in weakness, who, undaunted, when strength of body gives way throws himself in strength of soul and the humility of his finiteness on his sense of an overruling power in things that make for good. Here is the religious sense, in whatever words we may choose to clothe it, and at this point in the idea of life it must emerge for the healthy development, which is a mind-satisfying development, of human thought. Let us pause to consider this. The idea of life is not complete without reference to the common fact of personal failure in the pursuit of noble ends. How does this appear to the person who fails? How does it square with his idea of living for the end which he dies to attain, but does not attain? The human mind must have an answer to this question when its pressure in experience, real or imagined, reaches a certain point. There is no proof for the answer, except the proof that is implied in the question itself, and in the idea of life for a worthy end that lies behind it. But I do not think that a course of moral instruction is complete which does not, in some form or other, give the answer as the consciousness of man has given it from time immemorial. The creed may be made a very short one; it is this: "We believe that whatever was really good in the worthy man's aim will be accomplished though he has not accomplished it; and we believe that his life is not wasted, but the good of it survives in some way, even though he accomplished nothing that we can see." This, in its most abstract form, is that faith in God and Immortality which all the good old stories express in some simple concrete language, that, in my opinion, had better be left as it is to carry its own assurance somehow to the child's mind. But the teacher can suggest the application of its ethical meaning to common life, as a faith in the certain realization of all good ends and the immortal value of all good deeds. As regards the treatment further of the subject of religion, which here abuts so definitely on the subject of virtue, it depends so much on the family traditions of the learners, that I will not attempt to treat it generally here. I will only add the obvious reflection, that if the religious idea centres in these two ideas so much the better for its stability in after life.

I have referred to heroic literature as a storehouse of material for lessons on the moral ideal as we have so far considered it. So far as I know, the best for this purpose are the four antique literatures of Europe—Greek, Roman, Celtic, and Norse.

For the abstract idea of manly dignity, as consisting in the doing of deeds, and unflinching purpose in the face of obstacles, the Norse stories are most effective, and should be freely used, though certainly not exclusively for any length of time. The religious pessimism which lies behind them, and which nevertheless their heroism survives, supplies an additional nobility which should be noted, though, as too hard a saying, not of course insisted on. The other literatures have each a peculiar value of its own, and Celtic literature in particular has largely determined the character of mediaeval romance, and is the main source of the chivalrous ideal.

And this leads us to our second stage, which is marked in the history of the race by the development of the heroic ideal into the ideal of chivalry. Life for an object is life idealized barely, but a worthy life is for a worthy object. Life is worth living if there is something to live for, but what is the something that gives it most worth?

The answer to this question is a theory of life, and to that, briefly indicated, we shall come presently. But, first, we must consider the materials which human nature itself supplies for the construction of that theory.

What ends do we live for as a matter of fact? We aim at the preservation and increase of our own comfort and pleasure in a great variety of ways; we aim at carrying out our own ideas of whatever kind in the world. But we are not isolated individuals: our pleasures are bound up in a thousand ways with the pleasures and pains of others, and our ideas are affected by these and entangled with the ideas of others. We grow up in a social world, bound to it and to individuals in it by lively and passionate affections; our sympathies make us conscious of others as they are conscious of themselves, at least so far as to mitigate very practically the solitariness of our desires. There is no lack of ends to be served in a world like this. Human feeling twines itself round its objects of affection and makes their welfare part of its natural end. Thus comes the distinction between the self-seeker and him who prefers, within some vague wide limits, the good of others, or another. The latter is recognized as good, and approved. Some degree of consideration for others is required, or the man, however heroic, is blamed. The Norse stories again very aptly illustrate as a side issue this failure, and sometimes the hero himself has to acquire the gentler virtues in course of a painful experience. The finished hero in all literatures has them more or less. It is in their service that poetry and story first became moralized.

One class of tales teaches by showing how strength fails of loveliness and honour, when kindly affections, good faith, and hospitality are lacking. Another class sets forth these virtues in all their attractiveness, enhancing the effect perhaps by force of contrast with the churl, the treaty breaker, the inhospitable, the cruel man, the braggart, the inconstant friend. The strong man bears himself gently, restrains his strength and is kind; he conceals his powers and is modestly silent about himself; to strangers he is hospitable, to friends and country loyal, in enmity scrupulous to keep his treaties, in love constant and self-devoted. In all these ways the hero shows regard for others, and his great deeds shape themselves in reference to those duties to others which spring from his social character.

Celtic romance is a mine of concrete illustrations bearing on this ideal. In Dr. Joyce's collection of *Celtic Romances*, in Mr. Standish O'Grady's *Bardic History of Ireland*, and the charming little book by him called *Finn and his Friends*, there is abundant material. Besides the two great cycles of Irish story, the Ossianic and the Tan-bo, into which these books give us a glimpse, there are several detached stories of great beauty and use. There is also the more familiar cycle of the Arthurian romance, and its numerous adaptations in mediaeval tales of chivalry, the influence of which have permeated literature down to our own time.

In the chivalrous ideal the earlier barbarian heroic ideal is absorbed. Be strong of purpose it teaches, but gentle too, and use your strength for the service of those others who have a claim on you. Deal fairly with your enemy as you would that he should deal with you, and to those who have injured you be as generous as you can.

This last, however, is a counsel hard to the primitive man and late to be learned. Forgiveness has, indeed, been accounted a weakness and even a crime. In our day there are still those who cry out on "want of spirit" in persons who forgive slights and injuries easily—there are those who think it right to nurse their sense of wrong. Forgiveness, and the extension of charity to all men, were the two great lessons taught by Christianity to a Pagan world by no means deficient in other elements of virtue; but our Pagan world has found them very hard to learn and is struggling against the lesson still. This marks the third stage in the development of the child's moral ideal—the glow of universal friendliness, the grace of a forgiving mind. "Bless them that curse you, do good to them that hate you, and pray for them that despitefully use you and persecute you."

The gospel parables, the sermon on the mount, the story of Jesus—the lessons of meekness and charity can best be learned from the sources whence they come. A mind already awake to the conceptions of heroism is prepared to appreciate the magnanimity of the Christ-like character. "If thine enemy hunger, give him meat." "If ye love those that love you, what thank have ye?" Here then the New Testament becomes the main source of ideas; but other stories on which these noble conceptions have been grafted should also be used. In these days of books for children there are many beautiful renderings of old tales into which has been infused a larger spirit of Christian charity than originally pertained to them. And even in their most ancient guise many of the old romances have been deeply tinged with Christian feeling by the very conditions under which they have been handed down to our time. This is visibly true of the old Irish stories which were carefully written down, though apparently with much tender antiquarian sympathy, by the early monks, and it is obviously true of the Arthurian romance as we have it. The stories in the little book of Mr. Standish O'Grady's, already mentioned, are specially marked by the Christian spirit of forgiveness and charity. The stories in this case are modernized, but the same lessons occur in many of the antique tales, as, for instance, the meeting of the enemies at the end of the voyage of Maildun. It is wise, I think, to make the most of it when it occurs in a context of this kind, because readiness to forgive *as part of the heroic character* so obviously implies a victory over self which is all the nobler because the *conquered* self is not ignoble, that the conception is a peculiarly attractive one. It is the *finished* conception of the Christian knight—brave, resolute, and daring, gentle, modest, affectionate, and true, with a charity that knows no exceptions and a spirit to forgive even unto seventy times seven.

These Christian virtues are so difficult that no pains should be spared to secure that the idea of them shall be really grafted on the ideal of virtue in each child's mind as it already exists. He should see it not as an idea apart, but as part of the character he already admires,—in heroes of story, or great men, or whatever the bearers of the idea may happen to be for him. Hence it is necessary to bring home the lesson of the New Testament story, that story in general should be clothed in its conceptions. But this, of course, must be done with the reserve of art and skill, and the main stress of the teaching at this point is best, I think, laid on the Bible narrative itself. Moreover the learners should see, at least in their more advanced stage, the historical relation of the different parts of the ideal; and the influence of Christianity in softening and purifying the noblest conceptions to which our Pagan forefathers had attained should be traced and understood.

Having so far attained to the conception of a noble character wrought by perfect social feeling to noble ends, what lack we yet? Let us pause to consider the difficulties that might beset such a one as has been described, and the additional armour that he requires to cope with those difficulties.

In the first place he may fail—may prove that, good as he is in purpose, he is not resolutely good enough, or kind enough, to fulfil the law of love. This failure comes to us in three ways: either our strength fails, or some natural instinct takes possession of us and makes the right deed impossible, or we are not *good* enough—the moral spring of loving kindness is weak. Thus we do wrong, sometimes knowing it at the time, sometimes not till afterwards, and sometimes obstinately ignoring it even then. Those who are happily circumstanced, and happily dispositioned, both in strength and kindness, may long escape the fate of serious lapses; but none can be wholly spared who go out, as they should, to fight the evil in the world. The things alone that ought to be done and are not done count for much.

Now what is the true man's attitude when this happens to him. What idea shall we train in our children as the right idea of the wrongdoer relative to his deed. Nature herself answers us from all times and in all races:—he should be ashamed. He has broken away from the rule of the ideal—has falsified the prediction of his better self—has been faithless to the duty owing to another. He has sinned, and with the sin—the negation of duty, responsibility, conscience—comes the distinct personal realization of these. To feel the whole weight of the little word "ought" one must have experienced first the emphatic "ought not." Those on whom duty sits easily are those who have least *idea* of it. It is the break with the ideal that makes the strength of the ideal felt. And in the same way, if we turn to the subjective side of the experience, it is the consciousness of being, as the deed done bears witness, a person other than one took oneself to be, that brings into clear light conscience as the ideal of character, felt in all its might when roused by disobedience.

It would seem then that, if duty and conscience are to be realized as all-powerful over life—that is, if we are not to trust to mere good disposition, which would be to deny the value of moral instruction altogether—the sense of sin, shame, and repentance on wrong done, are essential parts of the moral ideal itself. This lesson we find in all literature, though nowhere is it taught with the same emphasis, intensity, and vigour as in the Hebrew Scriptures. Still it is a difficult lesson to teach or to learn well. It will not be learned if it be taught prematurely, for the sense of sin cannot precede the establishment of the ideal sinned against, though it does precede the full realization of the majesty of that ideal. And, again, it is difficult to learn because it is more difficult to see the beauty and fitness of shame and penitence than to see the beauty of the positive virtues themselves. Sackcloth and ashes are not in their nature heroic as valour and chivalry are. And, moreover, it is harder to own oneself wrong than even to forgive an injury.

It is at this point that I begin to feel the peculiar value of the Bible stories of the Old Testament, and the aspects of the ideal on which they lay stress. The modern world has drawn from the Hebrew Scriptures its uncompromising sense of duty as a personal good, and still more of character as a white robe of righteousness which it is terrible to soil; and, in doing so, it adds, as the Hebrews added, the duty of repentance as a part of its moral scheme—repentance in its twofold aspect of personal humiliation and the reparation, so far as possible, of wrong done.

Stories of real life are important here— stories that come quite closely home. The shame of the common lie, the shudder of self-contempt after unkind or foolish talk, the open apology for harsh words said, and all the little events of everyday wrong-doing should be treated from time to time—and not in all the lessons—as occasion serves, and with a view to make each little wanderer, *in esse* or *in posse*, take to himself the lesson that he requires.

In another way these lessons on wrong-doing are necessary, because so much petty wrong is done for lack of thought, against which provision might be made. The example that strikes one most forcibly is the repetition of a story reflecting discredit on somebody, and the ready credulity that accepts all such. It is by experience of wrong we learn how necessary it is, as a part of charity, to stop the harsh story when it reaches us until at least we have *ascertained* that it is true. Shame for the wrong done, in such and in other ways, to-day is the one safeguard that similar wrong will not be done to-morrow.

In the main, it may be said that the instruction which cultivates a penitent spirit is required, because the man who never finds occasion to repent is either like the Pharisee who measured himself amiss, or is not in earnest about the attainment of righteousness. No one can escape penitence who has his heart set on—not merely attracted by—the ideal of a life spotless in word and deed and thought, and who is at the same time a faithful critic of his own shortcomings. Thus that least attractive of all the virtues, a humble contrite heart, is but the inverse of that hunger and thirst for perfection which is the very bond of all good.

As the mind unfolds, the ideal of perfection slowly shapes itself in the child's mind, and draws his will into unity with it. There is a natural order in this development, and that teaching is most successful which, though without a doctrinaire artificiality, takes account of this order, and gives opportunities accordingly, in conversation, in reading, and in practice. First, admiration awakens for the hero as daring, resolute, and brave; secondly, this admiration glows the more tenderly for him as using his power chivalrously and for noble ends. Later, the ideal of Pagan chivalry leads up to the fuller ideals of a self-devotion without limit, a charity without flaw, a will set on good, and a vigilant conscience swift to chide.

CHAPTER V.

SUBJECT MATTER CONTINUED. SOCIAL MEMBERSHIP.

THERE is yet another theme that must detain us further, although it has been touched upon already. Our man of many virtues will meet with difficulties other than those of his moral limitations—coldness of heart and want of will. He will very often not know what he ought to do. This, like the difficulty of moral limitations, can never be quite surmounted. It stands in fact for the natural limit of human wisdom.

It can, however, be minimized—and the good man should so minimize it—by forming some theory, sound so far as it goes, of social welfare and the right relation of the individual to his fellows in society. Social good and social duty must be objects of study, at least in intention, to all who mean to live aright. For we may assume that the object of righteous conduct in the world is social good. Whether the sanction be conceived from a religious, or from a secular, point of view it directs us alike to the practical end of goodwill to men. In the moral education of children this end should, not be discussed, but tacitly assumed. Thus it will early dawn upon their consciousness that it is necessary to understand the conditions of human welfare, and the place of the individual in the whole.

For the little child it is enough that he should understand the family and its duties. Older children no doubt should begin to study the wider social circles in a simple way. But it is important to realize that the essence of social theory can be learnt from consideration of the family organization, supposing always that the family is large enough to illustrate the problem of divergent wills and their conciliation. The experience of the school organization is also of great value, and with reflection and observation on the family, and on the school, the seeds of the doctrine of true citizenship are not difficult to implant. It can easily be made obvious to young people that the law of the school exists for the common welfare, and in a well-governed family no other thought would be ever likely to arise in the minds of its members. It is curious how children—but girls more than boys—get into the habit of talking and thinking about "us" instead of "me."

It is not necessary for the present purpose that I should do more than touch briefly on the leading facts of social life and the principles underlying social welfare. The first obvious fact is that, of a number of persons living together, each has a tendency to take his own course—to do instinctively what he elects to do. But, apart from sympathy and reason, many persons have many ways, and these ways are sure to clash, so that the more each will tries to act freely the more all the divergent wills interfere with each other. Thus there is war and very little liberty, a state of affairs not unknown either in the nursery or in the drawing-room. Quite young children become familiar with this fact. It is part of moral instruction to train them to reflect upon it, its consequences, and their remedy.

Sympathy enables these divergent persons to understand each other, and prompts to ample concessions freely made. It is *reason*, however, that shows the *right direction* and *limits* of the concessions which ought to be made. To the reasonable mind it is obvious that of three little brothers or two brothers and a sister, the good of one is just as important as that of another. It is reasonable, therefore, to desire a system of things which secures, in the first place, whatever is recognized as good in common for them all, and, in the second place, fair-play between the three in other respects. We need not trouble the child, even if we think it worth while to trouble ourselves, with difficult questions as to the ultimate meaning of justice and fair-play. The simple, common-sense meaning is quite enough, viz. that the gain of one in any respect should not be considered—other things being equal—as more important than the gain of another. But it will be necessary to teach, as a part of fair-play, that those who are strongest and best endowed ought to claim less consideration than those who are feeble. The system of things which secures the good of all, and fair-play to each, is the law of the social circle; and the reasonable child sees the benefit of law to himself, as securing more real liberty for him in the long run. Moreover, he sees, unless blinded by selfishness, the benefit to his companions also. The latter benefit he values more the kindlier and more sympathetic he is.

It cannot be expected, however, that the child should understand all the regulations which put a circle of order round his life; nor, indeed, does the average adult citizen understand to the full the social mind that controls him. The wise child and the wise man know this, and think enough of others—and little enough of themselves—to be loyally obedient. This obedience is the auxiliary of reason, and almost a part of reason, in securing the social peace. It is in its essence at one with that prime principle of morality, the recognition of the moral law which should be obeyed. Obedience, the crude primitive virtue as we first met it, now reappears as marking the true citizen's acceptance of the social will.

Perfectly reasonable people are the law to themselves. All their wishes are consistent with it, and they are its source in so far as it is good. The imperfect reason in part accepts the law, as its law, and for the rest obeys. The unreasonable, however, are the persons for whom the law exists as a system of rules and discipline. If all were perfectly reasonable there would be no need for the formulae of such a system. The social will has to decree formally what *all* must do, because there are *some* who will not do it otherwise. Thus it appears that in a well-ordered society we are only unfree to the extent that we are unreasonable. The reasonable man is the free man in so far as the actual law of his society is a perfect law—that is, a law which *prevents* unreasonable persons from hindering the activity of those that are reasonable. But by what practical measures are they to be prevented? How, in the nursery, is the mischievous Jack to be prevented from breaking Dolly's toys? The children know that there are two ways. Jack may be told that, under penalty of some certain punishment, he is not to do this. This is the method of criminal law, and probably some criminal procedure, or at least the possibility of it, is necessary in every community of any size. By the other, and higher, method the unreasonable Jack may be persuaded to reason and consideration for others. This is the more excellent way, and in the family should be always what is *intended* in the end. The state of that nursery is bad indeed, where the naughty children are only kept in order, not trained to be eventually the source of order themselves. To the question who keeps order in the family, the answer ought to be that it is kept by all.

As in the nursery so in the world. The rule of the strong hand is necessary if only to enable the good citizen to go about his business. But this is no more than half the end proposed by a truly reasonable social will. The other half is to win *all* citizens to reason. Discipline, instruction, sympathy, persuasion, co-operation, are all means to this end, and they sufficiently define the attitude which ought to be taken by the individual good citizen towards those less advanced in social reason. It is his duty to help in winning them. The good little girl in the nursery makes it part of her business to bring her mischievous tyrannical brother to a gentler, more sympathetic, frame of mind. And, throughout life in all its relations, the duty of those who are injured by another consists in endeavouring to win that other to repentance by any means that will serve. The doctrine of forgiveness for injuries is a puzzling one to children as well as to men;

but it is not so difficult to understand it in this light, as a practical application of the principle that a brother remains a brother whether he offends or not, and that the aim of the good brother quite naturally is to persuade the other to a better mind. In all this department of moral teaching, the parallelism between the family, the school, and the world cannot be too carefully taught.

The relation of the good citizen to a law which does not easily fit him requires some consideration. Some laws exist to secure order and protect the peaceable by punishing ill-doers. This may lead to institutions which are occasionally oppressive, or at least troublesome, even to the good. A good citizen's duty in such case is to submit cheerfully, lest the weaker brother should offend. If his mind be fixed on the disciplinary benefit intended to those who need it, he will not rebel against an enactment unnecessary for himself. There is good occasion for this doctrine in the sixth form of the school.

In every society that the world has ever seen, the perfectly reasonable man has been in advance of the law under which his society is governed. It is sure to be inadequate to his view of what ought to be. It may be oppressive to him because of those enactments necessary for the discipline of others, or it may be positively wrong—a case which history amply illustrates. What is the good man's attitude in this latter case? This is a question which has been much discussed in the history of nonconformity. Probably it has been answered with the maximum of clearness by the Society of Friends, who have been placed again and again in the position of inquiring what are "the proper limits of obedience to the law." It is obviously absurd to say that disobedience is always wrong. It is obviously absurd, on the other hand, to say that we may disobey the law whenever we differ from its prescriptions. The happy mean was well struck by those who made it a principle of their political existence that the law should always be obeyed except *for conscience' sake.* This leaves the decision to the individual, it is true, but in such a way as to demand from him the highest exercise of responsible reflection before he presumes to differ from the powers that be. It should be noted too that such decision is necessarily made in face of the certainty that disobedience will bring suffering. Thus the Quaker rule was a wise rule which has acted well; although it does not follow that it should be regarded as an infallible first principle. Every case of disobedience to law should be judged on its own merits, and the lesson always clearly taught that an act of disobedience carries with it a tremendous responsibility which should never be undertaken except with a mind fully made up.

The same question comes up historically in another form, in all cases of national insurrection. The defence of the actual rebel differs from that of the mere non-juror. The former takes his stand, not only on the grounds of dissenting conscience, but also and more emphatically on the fact that the common-sense of his community is against the established state of things. This is a very strong position, since the duty of loyalty to institutions is grounded in the higher duty of loyalty to the common-sense and will of the community, or to superior persons claiming the rightful authority of true superiority. When, therefore, the general conscience is opposed to the established order, and recognizes no superiority in the persons upholding it, the higher duty, not only annuls, but opposes the other, and rebellion may become a sacred duty.

It is obvious too that a system of law will be best obeyed when it rests clearly on the will of the majority. Otherwise, there will be a larger number against than for it, and the condition must be one of unstable equilibrium. But where the will of the majority obtains there will be laws which enable the social will to override the individual will for the benefit of the whole. A majority is tyrannical that uses its power for the benefit of the majority only. The aim of all good law is for the benefit of the whole. In the discussion of such questions as those of local option and compulsory purchase, this principle may be abundantly illustrated.

These moral truths are taught most naturally in the study of history, but their application to everyday life should not be neglected, and history, with its lessons in high politics, will be better understood in the light of the comparison. It should be part, too, of the training of the young citizen to study in detail the political system under which he lives, and to apply his habits of ethical observation and reflection to it. It is a good sign of the times that a short course of lessons on the duties of a citizen is frequently given in schools to-day.

Such a course, however, should not be undertaken too early. Side by side with it, a short course of lessons on social and political principles in general would be useful, summing up and reducing to system the lessons on the subject hitherto given unsystematically and as occasion arose. To this might be added a course on economics, leading the learner into touch with the ideas of the industrial world. During school years, not much need be attempted for the full and detailed study of these subjects. But the cultivation of an interest in them and sympathy with the ends they imply, cannot easily be overestimated.

The chief object to be secured is that the young citizen shall thoroughly understand the principle of order under which he lives. Law exists, in the first place, for the protection of the perfectly reasonable citizen, that he may not be interfered with in carrying out his ends. In the second place, the law of the land is intended, up to a certain point, to promote the adoption of reasonable ways by all citizens. The good man, however, does not measure his duty by the requirements of the law. He owes more to his fellow-citizens, and will strive for the common welfare more than the law requires.

The course of lessons on the theory of social membership is not the least important part of moral instruction; for the end proposed in moral education is to train up, not only persons who respect themselves and feel with their neighbours, but citizens who honour the social order and accept the responsibility of making it all that it ought to be.

www.ingramcontent.com/pod-product-compliance
Lightning Source LLC
Chambersburg PA
CBHW030318170426
43202CB00009B/1054